Dear Cherry

✕ Questions and Answers on Eating Disorders

Cherry Boone O'Neill

CONTINUUM ✕ NEW YORK

1987
The Continuum Publishing Company
370 Lexington Avenue, New York, N.Y. 10017

Library of Congress Cataloging in Publication Data

O'Neill, Cherry Boone, 1954–
  Dear Cherry.

  Bibliography: p.
  1. Anorexia nervosa.   2. Bulimarexia.   I. Title.
RC552.A505   1985   616.85'2   85-4127
 ISBN 0-8264-0387-5 (pbk.)

This book is dedicated to those for whom answers came too late, whose questions were never heard, or perhaps, never asked.

It is written for the many who are currently struggling, asking for help, reaching out for hope, fighting for survival.

It is written with gratitude to those who have contributed to this project—those who wrote the letters, those whose insights and research have made answers possible, and finally, to my husband, Dan, for his continued help and support.

"We've only just begun to live . . ."

(Sung by Karen Carpenter)

Contents

Publisher's Preface

*I*n 1979 word began to circulate that Cherry Boone O'Neill had successfully conquered anorexia nervosa and bulimia, eating disorders which had threatened her life. At the same time, increasing news coverage began to spotlight the frightening proportions of what had apparently become a national epidemic of self-starvation.

Letters began to find their way to the O'Neill home, many with stories of hopelessness and desperation. Cherry answered them all personally with handwritten responses. She wanted to give the victims hope and encouragement in the midst of emotional pain and, in many cases, physical agony. On numerous occasions Cherry called hospitals to speak with girls barely clinging to life—for some, it marked the turning point in their recovery. But not for all. Some died.

In 1982 Cherry's book, *Starving for Attention,* quickly became a bestseller. Her harrowing narrative of illness and recovery inspired hundreds of thousands. No one had dared to expose their personal, private war with anorexia nervosa and bulimia in such stark, painful detail. The shocking, yet heartwarming story of victory brought a landslide of mail and phone calls to Dan and Cherry O'Neill. Appearances on the Today Show, Good Morning America, Phil Donahue and many other TV programs, as well as her interviews on radio and in periodicals, compounded the already heavy response by the public. Cherry had obviously touched a sensitive national nerve. Letters arrived from all over the United States, Canada, Europe, Asia, South America—even Australia and New Zealand.

So overwhelming has been the flow of mail that Cherry decided to share the correspondence, particularly those most frequently asked questions. This book is for everyone. We all know someone with an eating disorder. Cherry's experience and insight will help us to help others and to lead them to the care they so desperately need. This timely book is a hopeful, helpful collection of upbeat answers.

In the following sections Cherry shares some late medical opinions, discusses the genesis of this book project and presents written questions and answers which generally fall into the following categories: falling victim; families in conflict; the issue of control; perfectionism; mood disorders; getting help; getting well. Finally, concluding words of encouragement are followed by a comprehensive list of help sources and reading references.

Anorexia nervosa, bulimia and related eating disorders can be extremely dangerous to your health. Left untreated over a period of time, they can prove to be fatal. The author of this book is not practicing medicine or prescribing specific therapeutic measures but is providing encouragement and insights from personal experience. Both author and publisher wish to emphasize that persons who believe they may be afflicted with an eating disorder should immediately seek professional, medical help from experts qualified in the field.

Thoughts on Therapy

The past few years have seen a tremendous advance in the treatment of anorexia nervosa, bulimia and other related eating disorders. National publicity has helped to generate increasing interest in the field and it is becoming more apparent that the dimensions of the problem are greater than even many of the experts could have guessed. Although I do not claim to be an expert or scholar in this subject, I do read and attempt to keep in touch with developments through conversations with friends and medical authorities.

There are many studies and articles to be read, but one stands out in my mind.[1] It concludes that the occurrence of anorexia and bulimia are startlingly high. A confidential questionnaire was administered to three samples of students covering more than 1,000 individuals (two colleges and a secondary school). One percent to 4.2 percent of women met the specified criteria for a history of anorexia nervosa and an additional 6.5 percent to 18.6 percent showed a history of bulimia. To quote the article, ". . . prevalence rates appear substantial . . . these results augment the growing evidence that the eating disorders represent a serious public health

[1] H.G. Pope, J.I. Hudson, et al., "Prevalence of Anorexia Nervosa and Bulimia in Three Student Populations," *International Journal of Eating Disorders,* Spring 1984, vol. 3, no. 3.

problem." The following questions were used to score the respondents:

ANOREXIA NERVOSA

Response of "yes" required on both of the following two questions:

1. Have you ever had an intense fear of becoming obese?
2. Have you ever felt fat even when you were clearly below normal weight?

In addition, it was required that the individual have been at least 25 percent below ideal body weight at some time.

BULIMIA

Response of "yes" required on all of the following three questions:

1. Have you ever had episodes of binge eating, that is rapid consumption of a large amount of food in a discrete period of time, usually less than 2 hours? (If no, skip remaining questions.)
2. Do you consider the episodes an abnormal pattern of eating?
3. Do you generally feel depressed or down on yourself after a binge?

Response of "yes" required on three or more of the following five questions:

1. During binges, do you tend to eat high caloric, easily ingested foods?
2. Do you try to be inconspicuous during these episodes, so that others will not notice your eating?

3. Do the episodes ever continue without stopping until you experience abdominal pain, fall asleep, are interrupted by others, or deliberately make yourself vomit?
4. Some people go to great lengths to lose weight. Have you ever used laxatives, self-induced vomiting, or diuretics in order to lose weight?
5. Have you ever experienced weight fluctuations of greater than 10 pounds due to alternating binges and fasts?

Interestingly, of the 65 bulimic students, only 3.1 percent reported that they sought psychiatric help. Less than one third of the anorexic (or anorexic and bulimic) students sought psychiatric help. If there is any single theme which reoccurs through this compilation of letters and my replies, it is my repeated exhortation that those who fear they may fall into these categories go to qualified professionals for immediate help. I cannot overemphasize the importance of seeking this type of assistance. There are many of us who are alive today because of it.

What type of treatment might one expect? Eating disorders are terribly complex and each doctor will undoubtedly take a somewhat different approach but there are general conclusions which have been drawn regarding the primary issues to be dealt with in anorexia and bulimia. My own doctor, Raymond E. Vath, M.D., has outlined them as follows in his own approach to therapy:

1. Perfectionism: Among many victims there is a perceived need to have thoughts and behavior that are above reproach in order to avoid punishment or rejection. There is often a frantic striving to achieve.

2. Poor Self-image: Obviously, perfection is an impossible goal. When one dedicates themselves to attaining the unachievable, a sense of inadequacy and failure will be the logical consequence. Self-esteem drops and becomes part of the overall problem faced by the anorexic or bulimic.

3. Sexual Identity Confusion: Sometimes as a result of poor self-image, the gender role is rejected to some degree. There may be conscious or unconscious attempts to avoid sexual maturity due to fear or sexually frightening events of the past.

4. Depression: Any one or all of the above three problem areas may drive a person to feel that life is meaningless, hopeless and overwhelming. The patient feels sadness and anxiety and would like to give up. Anorexia, in this case, may become a slow form of suicide. Also, there may be genetic or biochemical bases for different types of depressions which have now been proven to contribute heavily in lives of many bulimics and anorexics.

5. Power Struggle: Conflicts often erupt as those around the anorexic attempt to stop them from their form of self-destruction. The tactics most frequently used are force, intimidation, guilt and manipulation which, in themselves, are often the very factors leading to perfectionism. The problem becomes worse instead of better.

6. Deception: Secretive eating, vomiting, denial, shoplifting and other behaviors are frequently adopted in order to avoid the power struggle. The deceptive behavior

may lead to relationship problems within families or marriages.

7. Dependency: A feeling of worthlessness, inadequacy and helplessness often results in a search for a protector. The patient may have decided to find another to take away their problem, fostering a kind of dependent posture.

8. Other Factors: There may be numerous other contributing factors, such as endocrine abnormalities which must be evaluated and considered in the therapeutic process.

Any one or all of the above issues may exist in a person's life and may require treatment. Dr. Vath feels strongly that this treatment should be a combination of family therapy (emphasizing cognitive therapy), medication (if necessary) and group support for the patient and family.

One of Dr. Vath's early clinical impressions in my own case centered around a mood disorder. Though this came as a surprise to us at the time, in retrospect the diagnosis was amazingly accurate and, subsequently, medication significantly impacted the disorder. Recent studies are continuing to confirm that mood disorders, particularly varying forms of depression, are at the heart of a significant percentage of eating disorder cases, especially bulimia. Two impressive works have emerged which include the role of depression and appropriate medication for bulimic patients. They also provide a sense of just how complex these disorders can be. *New Hope for Binge Eaters* by Harrison G. Pope and James I. Hudson (Harper & Row, 1984) is an excellent book on the subject (the reading gets a bit technical in places). "The

Syndrome of Bulimia: Review and Synthesis" by Craig Johnson not only deals with the mood disorder component of bulimia but echoes Dr. Vath's treatment formula of cognitive therapy, group interventions and antidepressant pharmacotherapy.[2]

Another vital area of concern being studied today is the potential for heart failure in the anorexic patient. Extreme care must be taken during the recovery process to avoid excessively rapid weight gain which could result in serious cardiac complications. In her article, "Heart Failure During Treatment of Anorexia Nervosa," Pauline S. Powers, M.D., cites starvation studies conducted during the 1940's in which 32 healthy young men underwent controlled semistarvation losing 25 percent of their body weight in six months.[3] After recovery, the researchers concluded from their observations "that the heart was actually relatively closer to failure in early rehabilitation than it was during starvation. They suggested that the heart, which was able to support the much lower basal metabolic load in late starvation and early rehabilitation, demonstrates its weakness when the metabolic demand is increased." Powers concludes her article with some practical recommendations:

1. Physical exercise should be kept to a minimum during recovery to avoid increasing the metabolic rate, in spite of objections by the patient.
2. Other patients on the ward should be informed about potential cardiac complications if weight gain is too quick or if bingeing occurs.

[2] Reprints are available by writing to: Dr. Craig Johnson, Northwestern Memorial Hospital, Institute of Psychiatry, 320 E. Huron, Chicago, IL 60611.
[3] *American Journal of Psychiatry* 139:9, 1982.

3. The patient should be monitored closely for cardiac status, including pulse, blood pressure, respiration, venous pressure, edema and related symptoms.
4. Periodic lab tests should include an ECG and measurements of calcium, magnesium and electrolyte levels.

This is one more important reason for expert medical care in treatment and recovery of seriously ill eating disorder victims. I personally know of several cases of fatal heart failure among recovering anorectic women.

In spite of all of the late findings and recent press coverage, those with eating disorders still belong to a generally secretive society. Accurate, hard data are difficult to come by. Generally, however, it is thought that those with the best prognosis for recovery are the younger patients. The best solution, of course, is prevention which may be enhanced by appropriate education on depression in society, self-image development in children, the teaching of conflict resolution skills (particularly in the family context) and the factors involved in perfectionism.

There is so much more to be learned about the causes and effects of anorexia nervosa and bulimia. However, many new insights, some of which I have mentioned here, have come to the surface and are of immeasurable help in saving lives and assisting in the healing process. In the Appendix the reader will find a listing of books, articles and sources of help for further inquiry.

Finally, there is the intangible yet undeniable inner force of hope. Without it, I could not have survived. Based on the breakthroughs, there is more reason for it now than ever before.

Introduction to the Letters

*I*t was with some trepidation that I awaited the official release of my first book, *Starving for Attention,* in the autumn of 1982. A year earlier, my husband, Dan, and I had discussed writing the story of my illness and recovery, knowing it would be a timely subject. We concluded that it was important that an autobiographical account of illness and recovery from an eating disorder be written and that it be an open, candid account. I can now identify with the person who once said, "Writing is easy—just sit down at a typewriter and open a vein." I found this to be a painful, yet rewarding project and one which produced an immediate and overwhelming response by readers.

Letters poured in by the bundle from nearly every state in the union as well as from Canada, England, Germany, Puerto Rico, Brazil, Japan, New Zealand, Australia, Greenland, Indonesia, Israel and other countries. They filled our home mailbox, Dan's office, were forwarded by our parents, sent through doctors, publishers, magazine editorial departments, television stations, radio disc jockeys and were often surreptitiously handed to me after speaking engagements around the country. They are desperate, painful epistles from stricken girls and women, their parents, husbands, brothers, sisters, boyfriends, girlfriends, roommates, relatives, and mere acquaintances. Many letters found their way to our home address bearing only my name and city.

At first I felt responsible—somehow obligated to rescue these victims as though I were their last link between life and death. Upon reflection, however, I realized that I was not ultimately accountable for anyone beyond myself, which freed me to pen uplifting notes and encouraging words of comfort. While I was able to attain a certain level of objective freedom in corresponding with desperate victims and their loved ones, I nevertheless maintained an underlying sense of urgency to personally respond to *each* letter, which I somehow managed in spite of a pressing schedule. Perhaps it was my own memory of desperation, fear and pain which provided the motivation to send replies to the many hundreds who have written. Just maybe, I thought to myself, these scraps of paper would become encouraging touchstones for many on their journey toward life and health. I had no one to write to in the midst of my own personal hell. A few lines from one who had conquered this nightmare would have meant so much to me.

The following letters contain a wide range of emotions, from the deepest despair to boundless elation, as the writers share their innermost hopes and fears. Their stories span the health spectrum from suicide to full recovery. It is my sincere desire that increased awareness of eating disorders, new advancements in therapy and these few sparks of hope will be a turning point for many in their quest for health and happiness.

Cherry Boone O'Neill

Letters

The author has changed the names and certain specific facts in letters represented in this book for the purpose of protecting the privacy of each correspondent. The author intends to convey encouragement to and inspire hope within all who read the following correspondence but wishes to emphasize the critical importance of consultation with qualified physicians when dealing with eating disorders.

Dear Cherry:

I have finally reached the point where I know I must reach out for help. I am terribly embarrassed and humiliated because earlier this week I was arrested by a store detective for shoplifting laxatives. I use them to help me lose weight, and although I have the money to buy them, I am embarrassed to buy so many at once. I am a prominent member of the community and word has gotten out already. I just pray this doesn't end up in the newspaper. But it has caused me to think seriously about my bulimia. Maybe it took this crisis for me to get up the nerve to actually write to you. Did you abuse laxatives or diuretics? How many did you take and how did you get off of them?

Muriel D.
Boulder, Colo.

Dear Muriel:

You have finally reached a point of crisis which is causing you to examine the real consequences of bulimic behavior. Be sure of this—there are many who are going through the same thing, so you are not alone. I can strongly identify, having gone through the same abuse of laxatives, which I consumed by the entire box on some occasions—over 60 pills at once! Your own situation has led you to see your actions more objectively even though your remorse may be more for having been caught than for the crime of shoplifting and perhaps more for having shoplifted than for abusing laxatives or being bulimic. But for whatever the reason, it is good that you are now reaching out for help. I kicked the laxative habit by simply stopping all consumption. I must admit that I was very uncomfortable with symptoms of bloating and constipation following this decision. While these are inevitable consequences, they are not permanent, which

23

should be of great comfort to you. I ate more roughage, bran, fruits and other appropriate foods to help my body function on its own rather than depending on laxatives. I must emphasize that the most important thing for you to do at this point in your life is to seek professional help before another more consequential crisis occurs. Consistent laxative or diuretic abuse can be extremely dangerous. Good luck!

Cherry

Dear Cherry and Dan:

You may remember meeting my husband and me last year at the White House at the Annual Washington Charity Dinner. You may recall we had a brief conversation about our daughter, Pamela, who was hospitalized at the time. Since that time, she has put on fifteen pounds and now weighs 114 at five feet six. By the way, you will be happy to know that she read your book in the hospital and says that you inspired her to "choose life." Here are my questions: Is it possible to *fully* recover from anorexia nervosa or is it like alcoholism? Did you have bizarre eating rituals and did they disappear after your recovery? Do you continue to exercise? We are hoping Pam is not in the midst of a relapse. Perhaps we are too sensitive. We would be thankful if you could give us your thoughts on these matters. Hopefully, the worst is behind us but I would be lying if I said we aren't a little worried.

Carolyn D.
Springfield, Mo.

Dear Carolyn:

Of course Dan and I remember meeting you and discussing your daughter's battle with anorexia nervosa. I can certainly tell you that it is possible to fully recover from this disorder although patience and a perseverent approach to the process of healing are required. While there seems to be some relationship between alcoholism and anorexia nervosa, there is a qualitative difference in the approach to recovery based on the fact that while it is possible to totally avoid alcohol, it is impossible to totally avoid food. In some ways this makes the anorexic's recovery more challenging because it is, for many people, more difficult to practice moderation than abstinence. The questions of eating rituals is certainly a relative one, because as individuals we oftentimes approach our meals differently. Who should decide what is normal? As my doctor said, there is nothing in the U. S. Constitution that says we should eat three square meals a day—morning, noon and night. It is very possible that during and after recovery, certain eating rituals will persist, although with many they seem to become less bizarre. What is most important is that Pam does that which is healthy and satisfying to her. I do continue to exercise approximately five to seven hours a week, a substantial drop from the six hours a day I once endured. Of course, exercise is important for everyone, but, again, it must be approached in moderation. Please greet Pam for me and let her know my prayers are with her.

Cherry O'Neill

ᕁᐟᐟ

Dear Mrs. O'Neill:

After reading your article in *McCall's Magazine*, I purchased your book and read it in one sitting—I couldn't put it down. I have a tremendous fear that our daughter (the youngest of three girls) may be becoming anorexic. She is only eleven years old but is extremely weight conscious and seems to exercise constantly. It is possible a girl of her age could have anorexia? She seems to eat well, but doesn't put on weight. Could she have bulimia? And what exactly is the difference between anorexia and bulimia?

Mrs. B. Larson
Miami, Fla.

Dear Mrs. Larson:

It is very possible that an eleven-year-old could be anorexic. I have traveled widely throughout the country lecturing on eating disorders and have encountered parents with children as young as six and seven who have been caught up in anorexia. I know girls whose eating disorders began between the ages of nine and eleven. I should also say that while anorexia nervosa was once called the disease of adolescent girls, it is now more prominent among older women as well, some of whom I have known in their forties and fifties. You say your daughter eats well but does not put on weight. This could be a sign of bulimia; however, oftentimes children this age are capable of burning calories at a high rate. Don't jump to conclusions yet, but keep a watchful eye on the following: psychological and emotional attitudes; signs of perfectionism; self-esteem; social interaction with her peers; substantial weight loss; approach to eating. Some have confused anorexia nervosa and bulimia. Anorexia nervosa literally means "nervous loss of appetite" which is a misnomer because frequently the appetite is as strong or stronger than ever. Anorexia is characterized by a severe abstinence from food, 20 to 25 percent body weight loss in a relatively short period and may be accompanied by an excessively rigorous exercise regimen. Bulimia, on the other hand, means "ox-like appetite." Again, this literal meaning may not be totally accurate because accompanying the inflated appetite is the uncontrolled gorging of food and subsequent purging activity which may take the form of vomiting and/or laxative use. Bulimarexia is a word which has been synthesized to include both anorexic and bulimic behavior and is typified by binge eating accompanied by the intense desire to avoid weight gain.

Cherry

ⅩⅭⅩⅭ

Dear Cherry:

I am writing to you because I feel lost, depressed and frightened after Karen Carpenter's death. She was my favorite singer and I have all of her records. I just can't believe it. I was surprised to hear she died of problems related to anorexia nervosa. I also suffer from that problem, although no one knows it. I read in *People* magazine that you were in contact with her before she died, is that true? I never thought of anorexia as being fatal. Do you have any words of advice?

Wendy T.
Boston, Mass.

Dear Wendy:

It is true that in the year preceding Karen Carpenter's untimely death, she reached out to me for help. We had several conversations by phone in which we discussed her disorder. I recommended a course of action which would move her out of the Hollywood environment, get her into professional therapy and I prepared her for the eventuality of a protracted healing period. Subsequently, Karen did move from Los Angeles, she did seek expert help, but she seemed to have had overly optimistic goals for recovery. Some have speculated she terminated her therapy too soon. The tragedy of Karen's death should serve as a warning that these kinds of eating disorders can be lethal. Indeed, there is a tremendous amount of interest in this subject, evidenced in what turned out to be the best-selling *People* magazine of 1983—Karen Carpenter's cover feature which reported her tragic death. Research which I did some years ago showed a 15 to 20 percent mortality rate, although it is extremely difficult to accurately determine the exact number of those with these types of eating disorders. It is nearly impossible to accurately analyze a secret society, so figures are still sketchy at best. We do know that there is a significant percentage of anorexics and bulimics who die or who suffer dangerous physical consequences. The main question I would put to you is this: do you truly want to get well? If so, seek help—the sooner the better!

Cherry

❧❧

Dear Cherry:

I hope you don't mind the fact that I'm writing to you even though you don't know who I am. I guess I feel I know you because I read your book and because Karen Carpenter mentioned you frequently. She told me she spoke with you about anorexia nervosa and she even showed me part of your book manuscript before *Starving for Attention* was published. We shared a hospital room together and we both seemed to be making progress in putting on weight. She seemed so happy and confident when she left the hospital—now she is dead and I feel I have lost a friend. I feel like I may be on the verge of a relapse. Has this ever happened to you? I hope you will have time to write to me but I will understand if you don't.

J. A. McCoy
New York, N.Y.

Dear Ms. McCoy:

As you undoubtedly know from conversations you apparently had with Karen, I spoke with her about my book. She seemed extremely interested in my own illness and subsequent recovery. I felt that it was important to share hope with those who simply needed that type of motivation to make the decision to get well. Of course we lost a friend in Karen when she died—the entire world did. She had much more music to share with us all. However, her death will not have been in vain if it served to motivate those in need of help to seek it earnestly. And yes, relapses can happen. If you read my book you'll see that I had my fair share of them. I should point out that I have not had a true relapse since I came out of therapy although the transition time during healing was, at times, shaky with limited setbacks. I feel that it is important to share with those in the recovery process that setbacks are to be expected. This is predictably difficult for perfectionists. I sometimes use the analogy of a withering tree with root disease. We might fertilize it, prune it, spray the leaves and perform other emergency techniques upon it. Unless the roots are properly dealt with, however, the tree is destined to die. For those who have truly dealt with the root, causal issues in their illnesses, relapse is highly unlikely. Don't give up— you can make it!

Cherry Boone O'Neill

≫ C ≫ C

Dear Cherry Boone O'Neill:

Last night I saw you on ABC's Nightline with Ted Koppel. It's about time we all learn more about the dangers of eating disorders. You came across extremely well. I just had to write and tell you about Tracy, our fifteen-year-old granddaughter. Six months ago she died after a three-year battle with anorexia nervosa. It was a tragic loss to us and to the entire family, as you can imagine. I know we can never have Tracy back again, but I want to thank you for writing your book with such honesty. I know it will comfort many to know that anorexia nervosa can be overcome. Many young lives will be saved because of you. I only wish Tracy could have read your book; it might have saved her life. Keep up the good work.

Mrs. Helen M.
Kirkland, Wash.

Dear Helen:

Thank you so much for your words of encouragement on my book and in regard to what some have called my "mission." It turns out, in retrospect, that the risks I was taking with my health were far greater than I was willing to admit at the time. Your letter serves to put us all on guard that anorexia is a potentially death-dealing malady which we must take seriously. It is possible that Tracy's passing may not have been in vain. From her death may come life as other sufferers are spurred on in a quest to conquer their illnesses. Thank you for your letter.

Cherry

✕ᴄ✕ᴄ

Dear Cherry Boone O'Neill:

After seeing you on the Phil Donahue Show and after reading your book, I found myself feeling resentment and anger. You had fame, money, a big home in Beverly Hills and a good doctor. You have a husband who loves you and now you are on all the talk shows. What about people like me? My parents are separated, I have no money and I just lost my job. I have no friends and no hope of recovery. It's so unfair. I'll bet you have a secretary who reads these letters and throws them away. If you write, I'll know you really care.

Gina S.
Boise, Idaho

Dear Gina:

Believe it or not, I have personally answered all mail which has come to me. While it has been an almost overwhelming task at times, I have felt that I should do all I can to share my message of encouragement and hope with those who are now suffering that which disabled me for nearly ten years. It is true that I was raised in a good family with substantial material blessings. My poverty, however, was in other areas. I had no real friends and, when it came to facing the full horror of my sickness, the material things did not help. In fact, they may have hindered me. In many ways I can certainly empathize with you where you are. It seems to me that you are harboring anger and hostility toward the world which, as you point out, can be so unfair. Your feelings will stunt your growth and hamper your healing, if left unreconciled, because they may stand in the way of the help and support you truly need. That help is out there, if you'll only pursue it diligently. I am pulling for you, Gina.

Cherry Boone O'Neill

P.S. I am enclosing a list of helpful reading materials and support groups. Please think about looking into them.*

* See Bibliography.

XCXC

Dear Cherry:

I saw you on Good Morning America talking about your struggle with anorexia nervosa and your recovery. I wish they would have given you more time! There are so many questions I want to ask. I developed anorexia at a very young age and I've had it for six years. (I'm now 17.) My father is with the Air Force and we have lived all over the world. It's been fun but also hard. I have no close friends and it seems that the friends I make I lose because we move so often. I don't feel that I have much to say in anything our family does. My father has threatened to put me in the hospital if I don't put on weight. He says I am just trying to get attention and if attention is what I want, he can arrange it with doctors who will force-feed me. I would die before I would let that happen! On television they said you wrote a book. What is the title and who publishes it? Did your parents also threaten to hospitalize you?

Lois A.
Tacoma, Wash.

Dear Lois:

My book is entitled *Starving for Attention* and was originally published in hardback form by The Continuum Publishing Company, New York. Subsequently, the book has come out in a paperback edition under the Dell imprint. If you read my story, you will find that some of the circumstances leading up to my illness are not dissimilar from your own. I am speaking of overwhelming circumstances over which we have little or no control. This leaves us grasping for an area of our lives which we may mold for ourselves and, for women, this frequently becomes our bodies. When this situation degenerates into a serious illness, such as anorexia nervosa, it is time to take steps to avert a health disaster. Remember that your parents love you—your father is a military man who, in his frustration, may want to take command of the situation through forced hospitalization. The best thing, of course, is not to let yourself get so thin that hospitalization becomes the only option. That is what happened to me. I was checked into Century City Hospital for approximately ten days because my weight had dropped to 80 pounds. I found that in the hospital what little control I possessed before was taken away from me. I would certainly recommend that you seek professional help. Conjoint family therapy would be the best option because it is within the context of the family that this illness develops and it is frequently through family involvement that we are able to come to terms with our illness. You will benefit and the family will benefit. Your parents will learn more of your views, everyone will learn to cope better and, hopefully, there will be a collaborative environment in which you may emerge from a dangerous illness. The best to you and your family— I will be thinking about you.

Cherry O'Neill

✗C✗C

Dear Cherry:

I just finished reading your book for the third time. I bought it after seeing you on the Phil Donahue Show. I know you say you have recovered but I have heard that it is extremely difficult and, in some cases, impossible to fully recover from anorexia nervosa. You still look very thin to me if you don't mind me saying so. How much do you weigh now? What was your lowest weight? Do you still exercise? How do you know you will not have another relapse?

Debbie W.
St. Paul, Minn.

Dear Debbie:

It is quite possible that I appeared thin on the Phil Donahue Show. I was fighting the flu and had embarked upon a grueling promotional tour across the country which took a few pounds off. At that time, I weighed around 110 pounds (my usual weight is 115). I'll admit that 110 pounds doesn't make me a heavyweight, but you will have to admit that it is tremendous progress over my all-time low of 80 pounds. Although I am not consumed with the desire to exercise excessively, I do put in a few hours a week of physical activity which makes me feel healthy and alert. I am quite certain that a relapse is out of the question for me because, at this time in my life, it would take a conscious choice to return to the inappropriate behavior of the past, and I'm not ready to make that choice—the cost is simply too high. Once the underlying causes of any illness are addressed, the symptoms will naturally abate. Although you don't write it in your letter, it would seem as though you may be suffering from an eating disorder. Seek the kind of help which will deal with the root problems of your condition and be prepared for healing to take time. It is a process—not a sudden event.

Cherry O'Neill

✂

Dear Cherry:

I find it hard to believe I'm actually writing to you admitting that I am bulimic. I have never shared this with anyone, not even my husband. For nine years I have binged and purged and I fear that this process has begun to take its toll. My teeth are damaged, I have broken blood vessels in my face, neck and around my eyes and, worst of all, I feel tremendous guilt. How can I ever tell my husband? He thinks we have a perfectly honest relationship. I know I need help but I fear that confessing everything may be more than Ron can take. I feel trapped. I read about you in your book and you are lucky to be married to someone like Dan. Any suggestions you have would be deeply appreciated. Please use the stamped envelope enclosed, which is not my home address.

Jane R.
Portland, Oreg.

Dear Jane:

I appreciate your honesty in admitting to me that you are battling with bulimia. Making that admission may be the first big step you take toward health–I know that was the case with me. Ultimately, you will have to share your condition with Ron so that he may be a true ally in the war you will wage to overcome this disorder. How you tell him is most important. Refrain from dumping it on him all at once. It is better to risk a little honesty at a time, testing the waters and starting the process toward full disclosure. He must have time to adjust to this revelation. After all, you must face the fact that it is entirely possible he could discover your bulimic activity at some future time, so beginning the process now will minimize the risk of confrontation and conflict. You may want to seek outside advice in the way of a doctor or support group which will help you determine ways in which you could approach your husband. You have obviously discovered the seriousness of bulimia—the consequences may be much more extreme if this disorder is allowed to continue unchecked. I know it will be a tough step to take and somewhat risky in terms of your marriage relationship but consider the alternatives. You have my full empathy and support as you start your walk on the road to good health! Let me know how things turn out.

Cherry Boone O'Neill

ᗢᗙ

Dear Cherry:

Undoubtedly you receive hundreds of letters, so I know I am simply one of many. After seeing you with Jane Pauley on the Today Show I thought I would take a chance that you might respond to our situation. I am thirty-five years old with a law practice in Los Angeles (we recently moved from Dallas). My wife is four years younger than I and suffers from anorexia and bulimia. She has become increasingly withdrawn and rarely leaves the house. Her weight has dropped more than ten pounds in the past three months to ninety-one pounds. Although I have caught her in the act of vomiting and taking laxatives, she refuses to admit that she is sick. It is impossible to discuss the relevant issues without bitter conflict. The cycle of bingeing, purging, lying, denial and confrontation has spanned more than six years and I'm not certain that our marriage will endure the stress. Our move to Los Angeles only seems to have made matters worse. I gave her your book which she refuses to read. Do you have any suggestions and would you consider writing her a letter urging her to seek help?

Vincent B.
Los Angeles, Calif.

Dear Vincent:

Your wife's refusal to admit to anorexic or bulimic behavior is quite typical and understandable. In the midst of her illness she fears rejection which would only compound her many problems. Withdrawal and social isolation are also common factors in the life of a person experiencing eating disorders. You really shouldn't feel guilty or responsible for your wife's problems but it would be extremely helpful if you were supportive of her during this time. If not threatened by rejection, she may indeed begin to reveal more about her illness and this kind of gradual admission is important in the overall healing process. Professional therapy is most important and should not be delayed. As her health improves, so will your marriage. It may not be the best idea for me to write to her at this point because she is denying the fact that she is ill. She may reject my letter in the same way she rejects the book. She cannot afford to acknowledge that she may have anorexia nervosa or bulimia. If, on the other hand, she writes to me I will respond. Let's hope for the best!

Cherry

❧❦❧

Dear Cherry:

I saw you with your family on the Donahue Show. We have been through so many of the same things. When Phil walked out at the close of the program with your beautiful little daughter, Brittany, I cried because I, too, am a recovered anorexic with a baby daughter. I am thankful to God and to my doctor for helping me through this terrible illness. I do have a question for you and I suppose you could say it is a fear which haunts me. Someday my daughter will be faced with the same pressures which caused my own illness.

What are you doing now and how do you plan to raise your little girl to make sure that she avoids this nightmare we both have gone through? Congratulations on your recovery and your successful book. I know you are helping many.

Gwen G.
Rochester, N.Y.

Dear Gwen:

Thank you for your letter and your comments about the television program and the book. It is sincerely my hope that many may experience inspiration and hope from my story. I must admit that from time to time I have stopped to utter a silent prayer that my children will never have to face the agony which I endured in the midst of my illness. I have prayed for the wisdom to utilize my experience in helping to shape the lives of my son and daughter. From a very early age it is important that we begin to instil self-confidence and a good self-image in our children. We must also resist the desire to excessively control or manipulate our children's lives. Though we may have good intentions, we may actually help to produce that which we fear. We must attempt to allow our children to explore, discover and grow into fulfilled, responsible persons. Ultimately, our goal should be to move toward the role of consultant, not authoritarian, as our children move into their teens. In allowing our children the opportunity to make some mistakes along life's road, we will hopefully avert the pitfall of creating perfectionists, whose goals can never be realized. It is a good idea to monitor eating habits but not to be forceful or overly strict in personal preference or style. Unquestionably, it is a tremendous challenge in today's world; however, there are a few simple steps we can take to avoid trouble along the way.

Cherry

⚜

Dear Cherry:

This is probably the first letter I have written in five years or maybe longer. I am hoping for a response from you, if at all possible. You may never have received a letter with problems like mine; I am frightened and ashamed; I cannot face going out of the house. I am depressed and there are many days when I do not get out of bed at all. My house is a terrible mess. I don't think of myself as an alcoholic, but my husband says that I am and that I should get help through Alcoholics Anonymous. On top of everything else, I think I am anorexic. I seem to have no appetite at all. Can alcoholism be related to anorexia? I really don't know if there is any hope for my condition, but after reading your book I convinced myself that there may be a way out of this awful mess. I am thirty-seven years old with no children. My husband has been so understanding but I know I've been a terrible burden to him. Do you honestly feel there is any hope in this situation?

Mrs. D. D.
Oakland, Calif.

Dear Mrs. D.:

If you truly have a fear of open spaces and leaving the confines of your home, you may have agoraphobia. Also, there are those who feel there may be a linkage between anorexia and alcoholism or bulimia and alcoholism. After what I have been through, I am an optimist. I truly believe that, even in the midst of your many problems, there is hope. It is definitely critical that you seek professional medical help in the form of psychotherapy if you desire to overcome the health challenges which are before you. You are most fortunate that you have an understanding, supportive husband. This will help you through the healing process toward recovery in many ways. Your depression may be an area of primary focus in bringing control to other areas of your life. There are different types of depression, some of which may be treated through therapy, others through appropriate prescription drugs, but it is imperative that you seek a professional medical opinion. Prepare to take some time in your journey toward improved health. As you know, there are no easy answers when it comes to alcoholism and eating disorders. It is good to know there is truly help available—I sincerely hope you will seek it!

Cherry O'Neill

✂✂

Dear Cherry:

Thank you so much for sharing your story in your book. It took a lot of courage to write about your life the way you did. I don't think I could be that honest, at least in such a public way. I also developed anorexia nervosa when I was about fifteen. I have had it for almost ten years. I was abused by my stepfather when I was in the sixth grade but I never told anyone about it. People seem to be talking more about sexual molestation now but back then things were kept quiet. The first boyfriend I ever had broke up with me because I wouldn't do what he wanted me to do. I feel these are terrible scars in my life and I know they had something to do with my current illness. Part of me says I would like to have a husband and children. But now I don't think that will be possible. I am five feet seven and weigh less than 100 pounds. If my weight goes above 100, I panic and do exercises like you did. Do you think I need a psychiatrist? I don't think of myself as being crazy.

S. Adams
Tulsa, Okla.

Dear Ms. Adams:

You are not alone! There are quite a number of girls suffering from anorexia nervosa who experienced some kind of trauma related to a sexual encounter. Don't think of yourself as being "crazy"—think of yourself as having been victimized, which is not a sin. It is something to be overcome through professional help over a period of time. The reason I would suggest psychiatric help is so that you may deal with your unfortunate experiences in such a way that they no longer force you into a cycle of self-destructiveness. A therapist, for example, may help you understand that because of your childhood experience with sexual abuse, you are subconsciously attempting to become less feminine and there-fore less attractive. Perhaps this is a kind of defense mechanism with which you hope to avoid future attacks of a similar nature. Once you are able to bring some perspective to these events, you will begin to successfully deal with your eating disorder. I know of others who have had experiences similar to yours who, with help from supportive family members and friends as well as professional counseling, have overcome their problems to live normal, happy lives. I sincerely hope this will be the case with you—good luck!

Cherry

⟫C⟫C

Dear Cherry O'Neill:

I saw you on a PBS late night talk show and I heard you interviewed on radio a short time later about your struggle with anorexia. I have exactly the opposite problem. I can't stop eating and the more depressed I get over my weight it seems the more I eat. You would never know that I was homecoming queen at my high school five years ago. Now I weigh 221 pounds. I have tried every diet and every pill. I cry myself to sleep at night thinking about it. You said in one of your interviews that many eating disorders are related. Do you think there may be common denominators between us which forced us in different directions? I am also the oldest of four girls and was a straight A student in high school. Help!

Maxine N.
Missoula, Mont.

Dear Maxine:

It sounds as though we have some things in common as you point out in your letter. Beyond the obvious academic success and family similarities, low self-esteem could well be a factor which drove us to food-related problems. Depression could be another and both of these factors could well require some professional medical expertise to sort out. You may want to look into Overeaters Anonymous—I have heard good things about this organization and there may be a chapter in your area. Prepare yourself for a process that will take time. These problems develop over a period of time and it should not be expected that they may be overcome quickly. After all, you know what they say about diamonds—it takes thousands of years to make one!

Cherry O'Neill

Dear Cherry:

You are the only person I know who is able to answer my question, so I'm taking a chance and writing to you. You may never read this, but I will feel better for writing it. I consider myself a recovered anorexic; not that I don't have occasional setbacks like everyone, but the worst is definitely behind me. My lowest weight was 89 pounds. I went through two years of therapy with a well-known psychiatrist who specializes in eating disorders. To be honest, I sometimes still battle bulimia but it is becoming less common. During my time of recovery I was married, and within one year I regained my period after four years of no monthly cycles at all. Well, I just found out for sure last week that I am pregnant. Of course we are happy but deep down inside I'm scared to death that the damage I did to my body may affect my unborn child. I have had terrible nightmares and although I am nearly recovered now, I feel more guilt than ever before because now my mistakes are going to directly affect another new life. After reading your book and seeing you on the Richard Simmons show with your beautiful little girl, I decided to ask you about how you faced pregnancy. Did you have these same fears? Did you have any complications and how much weight did you gain during your pregnancy? And what about morning sickness?

Mrs. T. C. McClure
Bakersfield, Calif.

P.S. I am 25 years old, 5 feet 5 and now weigh 114 pounds.

Dear Mrs. McClure:

As you have discovered, one of the many physiological consequences of a severe anorexic condition is amenorrhea (loss of menstrual cycle). There are some who will never recover their period and others, like us, who spontaneously menstruate when our bodies reach more normal levels of weight. In my case, there was no monthly cycle for more than seven years. I was terribly despondent that I might never bear children and that my husband would never experience the blessings of fatherhood. Now, I'm the mother of two healthy children. Like you, I was petrified for a few days after I found out I was pregnant in 1981. I would be less than honest if I didn't admit to the fact that there were fears I may have somehow damaged my body to the point that normal birth could be a question. As things turned out, however, I had a wonderful—even enjoyable—pregnancy and gave birth to a perfectly healthy girl. Although my second child, a boy, was born two months premature, my pregnancy was, nonetheless, quite normal. It is important that you focus on preparing yourself for a new addition to your family and that you treat your body well. After all, the way you treat yourself, during pregnancy, is the way you will be treating your unborn child. Fear and anxiety are more dangerous at this point in your life than other factors related to your pregnancy. Try to relax and look forward to motherhood. Unfortunately, morning sickness is one of those things which is unpredictable and a very possible consequence of pregnancy but should not be feared as a factor bearing on your child's health. If you have continuing doubts about your condition, confide in your doctor. Be sure to keep me posted!

Cherry

✄C✄C

Dear Cherry:

I hope this letter reaches you. . . . I don't even know if this is the right address, but here goes. After reading the newspaper article about your illness and your recovery, I bought your book and read it. The following week I saw you on the ABC news. It was then I knew I should write to you for help. I have never admitted to anyone that I am bulimic. It started last year when some of my girlfriends in our college dormitory taught me how to keep my weight down by getting rid of food following meals. Now I can't seem to stop and I know it's dangerous from what you said in your interview. Do I need medical help or is sheer willpower strong enough? Can you tell me what physical dangers there are in bulimic behavior? How do you control your appetite? I hope I'm not invading your privacy or asking too many questions, but I've reached the point where I know I must get help.

J. D. Parker
Detroit, Mich.

Dear J.:

Thank you for your honest letter. The fact that you have written to me is a step in the right direction toward admitting your problem and moving toward wellness. It is very common for bulimics to attempt to hide their eating disorder but the time must come when you will open up, at least to a doctor or another expert in eating disorders. By the way, I urge you to seek this kind of help at your earliest possible convenience because bulimia can be extremely dangerous with damage to your teeth (the constant flow of digestive juices over your enamel can cause it to erode away), stomach ailments, the rupture of blood vessels, damage to the esophagus, electrolyte imbalance and many other possible injuries. I would pass this warning along to your dormitory girlfriends who may be unaware of the danger of this kind of activity. There are surveys and studies which seem to indicate that there is a widespread epidemic of bulimic activity occurring primarily among women on college campuses across the nation. Regarding appetite, this can be a tremendous challenge to any recovering anorexic or bulimic. Because the delicate appestat mechanism has been abused over a period of time, it may take time to regain a true reading of appropriate levels of hunger or satiation. This is one of the consequences of eating disorders such as these, but should not necessarily be an enduring one. The bottom line is that you have decided conclusively that you must get help and that is the first step in conquering this problem. Best wishes to you.

Cherry Boone O'Neill

ꭓꮯꭓꮯ

My Dear Cherry:

I want to thank you for your book and for the many interviews you have done on eating disorders. It is now OK to talk about this problem, and this is mainly due to your loving and unselfish desire to help others by sharing your own story, difficult as that probably has been for you. Last year we lost our daughter, Bethany, to an overdose of barbiturates less than one month after she was released from the hospital. She was being treated for anorexia nervosa and had gained eleven pounds, which still put her well below the average weight for her height. She was never able to admit she had anorexia nervosa and never wanted us to speak about it, not even among relatives. Officially, she had "a gastro-intestinal disease." When she came home from the hospital, she was horrified to see herself in the mirror even though she weighed less than 100 pounds. We will never have our daughter back, but I believe others will live because of you. Thank you for your story and your honesty.

Mrs. T.J.D.
Virginia Beach, Va.

Dear Mrs. D.:

Thank you so much for the kind remarks about the work I am doing to shed light on the ever-increasing problems of anorexia nervosa and related eating disorders. I really feel it is time to get the story out. Unfortunately, this is not the first time I have heard of a young person choosing death over life, unable to face a distorted view of body image. Controlled scientific experimentation has demonstrated that persons with anorexia nervosa invariably and significantly overestimate the size of their bodies. They must be brought to new understanding of their problems and an awareness that help is available to them. There is no getting around the fact that Bethany's death is a tremendous tragedy to you and the many who knew her. My heart goes out to you and to numerous others who have lost loved ones to anorexia. The primary reason for going public with our story has been to provide a glimpse of the secret life of the anorexic and bulimic so that more light may be shed on the problem. Hopefully, this will encourage others to come forth for help. As you can imagine, it was not easy going into the painful details surrounding my own ten years of illness but we feel this will encourage honesty on the part of others. Thank you again for your comments—they are most encouraging.

Cherry O'Neill

ᗭᑕᗭᑕ

Dear Mrs. Boone O'Neill:

In April 1978 our daughter died of complications related to anorexia. Her life ended after two years of family turmoil and numerous attempts to deal with her problems through medical experts. This was a terrible blow to us, as you can imagine. But after seeing you on television and reading your story in a local magazine article, we decided to form a support group for anorexic girls. Now we know that Kathy's life—and her death—will count for something, even if only one girl recovers. Do you have any special thoughts or words of wisdom for us as we start this group? Thank you for taking time out of your busy schedule to reply.

Mr. and Mrs. W.
Denver, Colo.

Dear Mr. and Mrs. W.:

I applaud your dedication in starting a support group for victims of anorexia and bulimia. Indeed, Kathy's death will have tremendous meaning as others receive the help they so desperately need. It is going to be extremely important that you follow the proper guidelines in establishing your support group. First of all, I would highly recommend that you seek out other groups which have a track record of success and inquire about their programs. They will have much to offer in the way of experience. Secondly, I would recommend that you find an acknowledged expert in the field of eating disorders who would be willing to consult with you in establishing an effective program. Attempt to deal with the causes of eating disorders. Emotions, attitudes and feelings should be explored, not just the symptoms. It can be counterproductive to get into the details of inappropriate behavior because frequently patients will be tempted to compare methods and techniques of weight loss. You may also want to consider establishing a group encounter for friends and relatives of anorexics in order to better inform them of their support roles. I certainly wish you the best as you tackle a big challenge, but a most worthy one.

Cherry O'Neill

Dear Mrs. O'Neill:

I am nine years old. I am afraid I will be fat if I don't lose weight. My mother is overweight. I don't want to be like her, even though she is a nice person. I can't remember the name of your disease but we heard about it on TV. I wish I could have it for just one month. Or maybe one week. Are you fat now? Can you send me a picture of your family and please sign the picture.

Angela T.
San Diego, Calif.

Dear Angela:

Thank you for your letter. The name of my disease was anorexia nervosa. That's a pretty big word which means I had an eating problem. It is a very serious problem and one you never want to have—not for a month or even a week. It is an illness which needs a doctor's attention. I am not fat now but there was a time when I thought I was. At sixteen, I weighed about 140 pounds. I was just a little overweight, but in my mind I thought I was very, very fat. I didn't see myself right. So I tried to lose weight in the wrong way and that was the beginning of my serious problems in my life. The most important thing is that we find our ideal weight. This can take some time to do when we're growing up. Be careful about getting enough of the right kind of food and try to get daily exercise. If you still have problems and fears about your weight, you may want to talk to your family doctor. Enclosed is an autographed picture. God bless you!

Cherry Boone O'Neill

✘C✘C

Dear Cherry Boone:

You may have saved my life! I saw you on Hour Magazine with Gary Collins and was extremely moved by your story of recovery from self-starvation. For the first time I heard someone speaking directly to my problem; now I know there is help. I have decided to go to a psychiatrist who was recommended by our family doctor. My questions are related to exercise and weight: did you stop exercising (I am addicted to exercise—more than four hours a day). Also, exactly how many pounds do you feel I should put on? I am five feet four and weigh 96 pounds. My father says I should weigh no less than 110 pounds. How much do you weigh now?

Geri W.
Birmingham, Ala.

Dear Geri:

I am very pleased to hear that you have been motivated to reach out and seek the kind of help you really need. You are right—it may just have been a lifesaving decision! As you undoubtedly know, exercise is a disproportionately important part of an anorexic's life. Many victims of this disorder will go to incredible lengths to burn calories. I can remember when I was in the midst of my own problems, I would run ten miles while weighing less than 90 pounds! Exercise can, in fact, be somewhat addicting but it is important to scale back these activities to a moderate approach so that our health is maximized instead of threatened. Yes, I still exercise but not excessively. Now, if I miss an hour of swimming or an aerobic exercise session, I let it slip by without a second thought. In the midst of my illness, it was a very different story. I would double up on my exercise the following day, demanding far more of my body than was appropriate. Compulsive exercise while undernourished can do permanent damage to the body. Regarding a recommendation for weight gain, I would simply say that each person is different and should find their own weight for optimum health. Your father cannot say with absolute certainty that your weight should be 110 pounds. There is possibly a range of weights which would be comfortable and best for your bone structure. My own weight ranges from approximately 112 to 116 pounds. Give yourself some latitude and don't be excessively strict. It is possible that you may want to bring your family into a session or two with your doctor so that this matter may be discussed. I wish you well in your recovery process.

Cherry O'Neill

※C※C

Dear Cherry:

Back in 1976 I watched you and Dan on the Trinity Broadcasting Network. You talked about how you had anorexia nervosa in high school and college and you said you had recovered. After reading your story I now know that your troubles had hardly begun. Now, once again you seem to be certain that your eating and weight problems are all behind you. Are you really that confident? I feel that I have recovered, for the most part, but I have fears that I could backslide. How do you know when you are really cured?

Lou Ann S.
Tarzana, Calif.

Dear Lou Ann:

I knew it would catch up with me sooner or later! How well I remember that particular television interview program. I wanted so desperately to be well and to lay claim to perfect health. Indeed, I had made significant progress from earlier years, however, the underlying problems which helped to create my disorder had never been addressed in any real depth. I honestly thought, at that time, that I was close to being well. Not long after that program aired, as you know, I suffered a devastating relapse. My weight dropped to 80 pounds, I was hospitalized and would very possibly have died had I not received the expert help I needed to survive. Also, during that time I found it extremely difficult to admit errors, mistakes or weakness of any kind. That, in itself, was part of my problem. I had to be perfect. But we all know perfection is not attainable, therefore our goals are constantly frustrated which produces more interior stress. Now I am confident that I am fully recovered. I can say this with a conviction I did not possess in 1976 because now I understand the causes and roots of my illness. Once those factors were mastered, it was only a matter of time before I emerged from my crisis completely, although I should point out to you that an occasional setback is possible. It's good that you feel generally positive about your recovery. However, I would urge you to be sure that you understand why you became ill because after you come to understand the *why,* the *how* of recovery becomes much easier!

Cherry

⚜C⚜C

Dear Cherry Boone O'Neill:

Please forgive me for this intrusion. I'm sure you have more mail than you can answer. I am a thirty-six-year-old mother of two teenage children and I have suffered from anorexia nervosa and bulimia for what seems like an eternity.

It started when I was in college. When I finally worked up the nerve to see a psychiatrist he said, "Relax, honey, and try to eat like everyone else." I went away more depressed than before. My condition is now worsening and I am missing days at work. I keep all the books for my husband's construction company and so I cannot be hospitalized for illness. I am in a no-win situation and it seems there is no way out. Thank you for listening to me and if you could possibly spare the time, I would appreciate a letter but will understand if this is impossible for you. I heard about you through an anorexia support group when our family went on vacation in Los Angeles last summer.

Betty T.
Raleigh, N.C.

Dear Betty:

As I tell most everyone who writes me, anyone suffering from anorexia nervosa and bulimia must receive competent, professional help. Judging from the response of your psychiatrist, I would say that you are seeing the wrong person. Therefore, my first recommendation is that you search out an acknowledged expert in the field of eating disorders. Sufferers of anorexia nervosa frequently live their lives for others while neglecting their own personal needs. They tend to be people-pleasers and this would seem to be the case with your work. It's true, your husband's construction company is important, and it is good that you feel a loyalty to continue; however, your first priority must be to protect the company's assets—and you are one of them! I am assuming your husband knows something of the health challenges you are facing, in which case you should have a serious discussion with him about tending to your basic need for survival. Perhaps you could work out a compromise between therapy and work hours which would be acceptable to everyone involved.

Cherry O'Neill

✗C✗C

Dear Cherry:

I hope and pray that by the time this letter reaches you our daughter is still alive. She is currently in the hospital where she has been for months. She weighs less than 75 pounds. (In one year she lost more than 45 pounds.) Marilyn is not herself. She seems to want to die, although she never says it in those words. In the past two days she has ripped the tubes out of her arms which are now her only means of nutrition. We never dreamed things could become this bad in our worst nightmares. My husband and I read your book together. I don't know how many times we looked at one another, seeing ourselves and our daughter in those pages. I know I am imposing on you, but we love our daughter so much and we don't want her to die. Could you write her a brief note of encouragement? We would give her your book, but her eyesight is failing and I honestly don't feel she would finish it. We are hoping and praying.

Mr. and Mrs. Lanny K.
Thousand Oaks, Calif.

Dear Mr. and Mrs. K.:

I received your letter just this morning and because of the apparent urgency of your situation I am going to get this off to you as soon as possible. When you said that at 75 pounds Marilyn is not herself, you were exactly right. She has starved herself to the point where she is not thinking coherently or logically. This is very common among anorexics who have let their weight drop to starvation levels. As you may know, my own weight dropped to 80 pounds at one point and I was hospitalized for a period of time. I know there was a part of me that did not want to go on living, but underneath it all I really wanted to survive and live happily. I must believe this is the case with Marilyn. Please find enclosed a note to her which you may give to her when you next visit the hospital. My thoughts and prayers are with you.

Cherry Boone O'Neill

Dear Marilyn:

Your parents have shared with me something of your situation. I am one who understands where you are because I lived there for years. There were times when I cried out to God to take my life because my own circumstances had become so confused, desperate and seemingly hopeless that I did not want to go on. I seemed to be hurting myself and everyone else. Death seemed like the only way out. But there is something in all of us that wants to live—to survive. I reached the point in my life where I simply had to trust others to help me because my own vision was so clouded and darkened. That's what you must do now with those who are sustaining your life. Give them some cooperation and give yourself a chance, because I know you will be thankful later on. There are those around you who love you very much and, given the time, you will eventually even love yourself. I am going to ask you to do me a very special favor. As difficult as it may be, accept the help of those around you and allow yourself to gain a few pounds and gain a bit more time. Allow yourself some space to reconsider and to choose life over death. Ultimately, of course, you must bear responsibility for your own life—for your own decisions. I am simply asking you to trust those around you who care and who know what they are doing. Will you do me that favor? I am praying for you.

Cherry Boone O'Neill

✕C✕C

Dear Cherry Boone O'Neill:

I know you are probably very busy so I'll try to make this short. After suffering quietly and secretly with anorexia nervosa and bulimia for several years, I finally gave in to my husband's advice that I see a psychiatrist. In fact, he threatened to leave me if I didn't get help, and I know I don't want a divorce, even though our marriage has been full of problems for years. With the help of this doctor, I was able to overcome anorexia. What I mean is, I put on enough weight so that you wouldn't call me skinny. (I now weigh 113 pounds.) But I have not overcome bulimia, in fact, it seems to have gotten worse. I grew terribly dependent upon my doctor. He was so loving and so patient with me through all of my ups and downs. Well, to everyone's shock, he committed suicide a few days ago. It doesn't seem possible that a man with such understanding could do such a thing. And now I feel I've lost the only person in the entire world who fully understood my problem and could really offer me help. I feel numb with grief and depression and already I can feel the panic beginning to set in. I'm afraid to find another doctor and start the process all over again. I really, honestly, don't know what to do. Is there any chance at all that you could write to me? Just hearing from you would be a great help. My doctor said your book was one of the best personal stories of experiencing and recovering from an eating disorder that he had ever read.

Cheri W.
Philadelphia, Pa.

Dear Cheri:

Your grief reaction to the death of your doctor is very understandable. He was obviously a source of strength and a guide in your healing process, and there is no getting around the fact that his passing is a tremendous loss to you in many ways. It is important to realize, though, that your healing ultimately depends upon you, not someone else. Frequently, in a doctor/patient relationship, excessive levels of dependence are built up which leave us vulnerable. There are some who believe that in order to assist the anorexic or bulimic, the patient must become dependent upon the doctor so he may lead her through the process of getting well. I question this practice because we can sometimes end up trading one problem for another. Anorexics tend to be dependent—I believe they should be helped to be more independent. In overcoming the pain of your loss, attempt to honor the memory of your doctor by capitalizing on the good advice he gave you and see this as a new opportunity to step out on your own a bit more. If problems persist, it would be a good idea to find another therapist who may just shed new light on the old problem. Also, Cheri, I would encourage you to involve your husband in building a supportive relationship which will build-in a source of strength and collaboration in dealing with your recovery process.

Cherry Boone O'Neill

ᚷᚷ

Dear Cherry:

I know from your book that you are deeply committed to your Christian faith. I'm sure that this is what helped you through your hard times, don't you agree? We have a problem concerning the therapist that has been recommended for our nineteen-year-old daughter, Cindy. He is reputed to be an expert in the area of eating disorders and family relationships. We know, however, that he is not a religious person and probably doesn't believe in God. My husband and I have resisted going to him for that reason but we would be willing to give it a second thought if you have some ideas in this regard.

Mr. and Mrs. D. Donaldson
Olympia, Wash.

Dear Mr. and Mrs. Donaldson:

I definitely understand your desire to find a doctor who is philosophically and theologically compatible with your own world view. I know this was extremely important to me, however, I think there are some other considerations to be weighed. Obviously, it is not always convenient or even possible to locate one who fits your religious background perfectly. It is therefore important for you to understand that much of the knowledge surrounding anorexia nervosa involves objective, scientific fact which has nothing to do with religious beliefs. There are certain common denominators and principles which doctors understand and can apply independently of belief systems. Sometimes I use the following example. You are driving down the freeway and your car breaks down, which of course means you are going to make a telephone call for help. Do you call your minister or do you call a qualified automobile mechanic? I think you know the answer. The medical profession has made great leaps forward in recent years regarding the causes and treatment for anorexia nervosa. I would urge you to make an appointment with the therapist in question and frankly share with him your concerns. Please convey my greetings to Cindy and best wishes for a positive recovery.

Cherry

✠✠

Dear Cherry:

I am trying to lose weight, but I am trying to do it the right way. I do not use laxatives or vomiting techniques which some of my friends use. I am able to go for days at a time with no food. Sometimes I feel a little dizzy, but I don't seem to have any ill effects. My friends all say I have lost enough weight but I think they are determined to see me fail in my desire to get down to 100 pounds. No one knows how I feel inside. When I was in the eighth grade I had a weight problem and weighed 135 pounds. My teacher told me I was eating too much and that I should try to control my weight. Now that I am trying to do the right thing people are saying that I have gone too far. I told my friends I would write to you because you are an expert on weight problems. What do you think?

Jessica L.
Simi Valley, Calif.

Dear Jessica:

It would seem to me from your letter that you are extremely preoccupied with your weight. This could indicate that there are problems in the making, however, there is no clear line which one must cross to be classified anorexic. There are phases and ranges of neurotic behavior and no one has dared to split hairs or ounces on where normalcy leaves off and the neurosis picks up. I understand how you felt at 135 pounds because that is about what I weighed in the tenth grade. I, too, felt extremely self-conscious and demoralized over what I perceived to be a crisis in my life. I would highly recommend that you talk to someone who can give you some objective advice, perhaps a school counselor or your family doctor. They will give you recommendations for safe dieting and honest feedback about your weight and appearance. Remember that what is on the inside is far more important than what we see on the outside. A good self-image will take you a long way toward attaining the goals you have for life.

Cherry

✃✃

Dear Cherry:

I remember when you were born! I watched your father on the Arthur Godfrey Show. He is one of my favorite singers. I am writing to you to request some information on anorexia nervosa. Is it possible for men and boys to have this disease? I am extremely worried about my grandson who graduated from high school last year. He has a very low self-image even though his grades were among the highest in his class. He has always been impatient with his shortcomings. He doesn't exercise as apparently most anorexics do, and I don't believe he engages in bulimic behavior but he almost never eats. He is five feet nine and cannot weigh more than 120 pounds—maybe less. Should I say something to him? How much weight must one lose before they are diagnosed as anorexic? He refuses to discuss the problem with his parents.

Mrs. H. Perry
Great Falls, Mont.

Dear Mrs. Perry:

It is possible for a male to have anorexia nervosa although it is relatively uncommon as compared with girls and women. Between 5 and 10 percent of anorexics are male. It is possible, given the evidence, that your grandson could be anorexic. A typical anorexic will lose around 25 percent of their body weight. At 120 pounds he could be a borderline case. If you feel your relationship with your grandson is an uplifting and positive one, perhaps you may risk broaching the subject of his condition. If he resists discussion of the matter, it would be best to discuss other areas of his life that will allow you to see whether or not he is dissatisfied or generally upset. The most important thing is to be available and supportive.

Cherry O'Neill

⚜

Dear Cherry Boone:

You are my favorite of the Boone girls. I have your record albums. My favorite song is "You Light Up My Life" by Debby. My second favorite song is "Just a Matter of Time" on Debby's *You Light Up My Life* album. I liked it even before I knew that you wrote the song. Our family saw you perform at Knott's Berry Farm a few summers ago. You didn't look sick to me. Did you try to hide your sickness? How could you be that sick and still do all of the things you did? Do you still perform with your family?

Shelly R.
Tustin, Calif.

Dear Shelly:

Thank you for your very complimentary letter. I am encouraged to hear that you have enjoyed our music and performances over the years. When you saw me perform on stage, I was indeed suffering from anorexia nervosa. I did a good job of covering it up with makeup and layers of clothing. Most of us, particularly anorexics, do not desire to allow weaknesses or shortcomings to be seen. I was no exception. Anorexics are usually people of tremendous self-discipline and powerful motivation so it is no wonder that they seem to maintain high energy lives, which was definitely the case with me. Of course, this cannot continue indefinitely because the natural consequences of starvation will take its devastating toll. If you had seen me a year later, you would have seen a depressed and broken person. As far as show business is concerned, we now rarely perform together as a family, however, each of us has specific areas of interest in music, recording, television, publishing or other types of media involvement.

Cherry O'Neill

✕C✕C

Dear Cherry:

I watched the PTL television program where you talked about your hospitalization and recovery. I had never heard of anorexia nervosa until this year when my beautiful young niece, Tina, came down with it. I have no children of my own so Tina has been very precious to me. She is thirteen years old and her parents are terribly worried that she could be permanently damaging herself. They know all about your story but are hesitant to write to you. So, here I am! If this letter reaches you, please send a few words of encouragement.

Tina's father has been seeing a psychoanalyst for several years. Do you think it's a good idea for Tina to go also? God bless you for the tremendous work you are doing.

Jean P.
Sacramento, Calif.

Dear Jean:

I am sorry to hear that your niece, Tina, is suffering from anorexia nervosa. It is true that permanent damage can be sustained from this disorder, particularly if it endures over a period of years. So now is the time to start treatment, not later. I have had a number of people ask about psychoanalysis and, at the risk of sticking my neck out a bit, I will make a couple of comments. First of all, psychoanalysis is sometimes a very protracted analytical approach to problems. It tends to be rather nondirective. On the other hand, psychotherapy tends to move a person beyond understanding the problem toward conquering the problem. A therapist is one who works with a patient to clarify choices and options so that real progress may be made in establishing a healthy course of action. It is for these reasons that I suggest psychotherapy, especially for a person of this age. In fact, it's very important for a person of any age. I sincerely hope that Tina will receive the help she needs to conquer her problem.

Cherry O'Neill

꘎꘏

Dear Mrs. O'Neill:

When you were in Nashville speaking at a hospital conference, my sister invited me to attend. At first I said I would but then I backed out at the last minute. I was afraid to go and have people see me. I have anorexia nervosa. The last time I weighed my weight was 89 pounds and I know I have lost more weight since that time. My sister, Jana, was very impressed with your presentation. She bought one of your books and gave it to me. Now I am sorry I missed the conference. I don't know where to turn and I think that I'm ready for help. I'm tired of being sick, but I'm afraid to put on weight. Any weight I put on is always flab. If I must put on weight, I want to put on the right kind of weight. How fast did you gain weight and how did you keep from getting fat? I am in my senior year of high school.

Becky T.
Nashville, Tenn.

P.S. Jana's best friend, Darlene, goes to the same church as your grandparents here in Nashville. Will you be coming to Nashville again soon?

Dear Becky:

It is unfortunate that we missed one another at my Nashville appearance. I frequently have the opportunity, during such engagements, to talk personally with those who are undergoing the trials of eating disorders. Please don't let the fact that you missed the conference keep you from seeking the kind of expert help you need. It sounds to me that your weight is down in the danger zone and I would urge you to take that first positive step toward getting well. Like you, I reached a point in my life where I was sick and tired of being sick and tired. My greatest fear was that I would put on weight, yet I knew that was precisely what I needed to do to live. It was the hardest decision of my life but the payoff was worth it in every respect. My greatest fear in putting on weight was that it would be "the wrong kind." I was deathly afraid of putting on flab when I really wanted tough, highly toned muscle. I overlooked the fact that all our bodies need a certain amount of adipose tissue—in simple language it is called fat! We must have a certain amount for survival and, as women, we need it to perpetuate our female functions. I strongly suggest that you put on some weight knowing that some of it will, in fact, be fat. Later, after you have attained a level of strength and better health, you can use exercise and body toning techniques to keep yourself in shape. Regarding the duration of my weight gain program, the pounds came on very slowly. Although many of our friends and relatives would like to see quicker results, a fast weight gain program can actually lead to problems by overtaxing the cardiovascular system. Remember, the heart is a muscle and experts in malnutrition will tell you that this muscle will atrophy and lose strength the same as the rest of the body if we are deprived of food over a period of time. Therefore, take it easy, relax and allow yourself to gain weight just a little at a time. At least you are establishing a positive direction in the healing process.

Cherry O'Neill

Dear Cherry:

This is kind of an embarrassing letter to write, but here goes. I had a bad sexual experience with a boyfriend in my junior year of high school. I think this might have led to my becoming anorexic. I couldn't face the idea of sex. That has slowly changed over the years and now I am married. Now my husband says I look repulsive—he calls me a refugee—because I am too thin for his liking. He says it turns him off. It's gotten to the point that our marriage is in serious trouble. We went to a marriage counselor but he says until I get help for my own illness we are just wasting our money on him. I weigh 102 pounds and I am five feet five inches tall. My husband says I should weigh 125 pounds, at least! What is your opinion?

Susan K.
Los Angeles, Calif.

Dear Susan:

Don't feel embarrassed or alone. It is very common that girls suffering from anorexia have experienced a negative sexual encounter in their adolescent years. Even the smallest comment or transgression may affect an overly sensitive person to the point of developing an eating disorder. In a relationship such as yours, it is always important to empathize with the other person. You can't blame your husband for admitting that you are unattractive if you are excessively thin. You must weigh his sentiments against your desire to hang on to thinness, knowing that you may not be able to have both. I would tend to agree with your marriage counselor in that his ability to help your relationship will be severely limited if your own problem with body image is not dealt with on a priority basis. It is for this reason that I would suggest that you find an acknowledged expert in the field of eating disorders to work this problem through with you. I have a hunch that as you get a handle on your anorexia, your marriage will begin to experience the benefits. I cannot tell you exactly how much you should weigh, but I can tell you that at this time, the exact numbers are not as important as your willingness to confront the problem. By the way, it would be a good idea to involve your husband in any therapy sessions you have so that he may come to more fully understand your illness and its causes.

Cherry

❧C❧C

Dear Cherry:

How can I ever thank you for taking time to call me in the hospital. My parents said they would try to contact you but I never thought they would. They talked to your husband, Dan, and he gave you my phone number. I was so surprised I didn't know what to say. I know I must have sounded stupid. Now there are so many questions I could have asked you. I'm out of the hospital now and I feel much better about myself, but I am still frightened when I see the pounds going on. I am especially concerned because I am getting bloated. My doctor says this is a normal part of recovering from malnutrition, but I think he is just saying that to make me feel better. Did you go through this? Thank you for your encouragement and taking the time to reach out to me.

Theresa M.
Little Rock, Ark.

Dear Theresa:

I am so glad to hear that you are finally out of the hospital and feeling good about yourself. It is natural that you should be experiencing doubts and fears about the weight which you are putting on, but this is all part of the healing process. I went through it myself and I can also add that the bloating that you are experiencing is to be expected but it will not continue. For the severely underweight person, this bloating may be caused by gas generated by incomplete digestion of food in the stomach due to an imbalance in juices needed for digestion. This is the result of self-starvation—you have probably seen the bloated bellies of children who are mal-nourished in third world countries. Also, during the recovery process there may be a certain amount of water retention which can also cause bloating and some discomfort. But, again, this is a temporary condition of which you should keep your doctor apprised. I am always careful to point out,

Theresa, that it is a joy to be able to put this kind of illness behind you, but there are always stumbling blocks and challenges along the way. In the long run, this can strengthen you even though the temporary discomfort experienced can cause doubts and fears. I know you'll make it!

Cherry Boone O'Neill

ᕽᑕᕽᑕ

Dear Cherry:

If there is anyone who can understand my predicament it would be you. Your book gave me the strength I needed to seek treatment for anorexia nervosa. I went to see a psychiatrist who was very helpful. My husband came to as many sessions as he could, but my parents refused to attend saying that psychiatrists always blame the parents for the problems of their children. What has made matters worse is that many of my problems did come from my strict upbringing and my mother's overprotectiveness. To make a long story short, my marriage is better than it ever has been, my health is greatly improved but my relationship with my parents may be irreparably damaged. If you were me, how would you approach this problem knowing that your parents helped to create the illness but also knowing that you want to have a good relationship with them?

Mary Ann V.
Spokane, Wash.

Dear Mary Ann:

Thank you for giving some feedback about the influence my story has had on your life. It is always rewarding to hear of the victories. The family problems you are encountering in therapy are not unique, in fact, I experienced some of the same touchy issues. It is very beneficial to have had your husband in on your therapy sessions. This will build the bond of understanding and trust between you and create the supportiveness you will need to persist in attaining your health goals. Because eating disorders, particularly anorexia nervosa, are formed within the context of the family unit as we grow up, it is usually important to have parental involvement if at all possible. It is understandable that your parents are reacting to the fears that blame is going to be placed upon them for your illness. But this is where you must speak openly and frankly about your feelings at this point in your life. You can be confronting, yet at the same time loving. You should also reassure them that the goal of therapy is not to place blame, but to explore events and feelings in our lives which have created certain preconditions to illness. I have a good idea that if your therapist is aware of your parent's fears, he will make a special attempt to welcome them to dialogue in conjoint sessions in a nonthreatening way. An important step for you to take could be offering forgiveness to your mother for what you perceive to have been her overprotective qualities. You may tell her that you know it was out of love and maternal care that she behaved in this manner and that you understand her simple desire to be a good mother. It is possible there are also events in your own life for which you may want to ask forgiveness. This can be an extremely disarming approach and one which could inaugurate a new level of relationship between you. Life is too short for us to be harboring bitterness toward one another, particularly within the family unit. I trust all will go well with yours.

Cherry

〜

Dear Cherry:

Your book was assigned reading for one of our classes in school. It was a very good book. I can't believe all you went through! Some of us would like to know what you're doing now. Do you still appear on television? What does your husband do? Do you have children? How do you spend most of your time now?

Candy M.
Everett, Wash.

Dear Candy:

Thank you for your letter and for your comments on my book. I truly hope that you and your friends learned something about the seriousness of eating disorders. You may have heard the phrase, "forewarned is forearmed." At the present time my life consists primarily of being a housewife and mother, which I thoroughly enjoy. I have a little girl named Brittany, three years old, and a son, Brendan, one. They are extremely active so my work is cut out for me! From time to time, I will travel to attend a conference or speaking engagement and once in a while I will do a television or radio interview, which usually relates to the nationwide problem of eating disorders and how I recovered from mine. I am also very involved with the Easter Seals yearly telethon which raises funds for the disabled. My husband, Dan, is a co-founder and Chairman of the Board of Mercy Corps International, an organization to feed, clothe and shelter poor people and refugees in various parts of the world. He is also an author. I hope this answers your questions—say hello to your friends for me!

Cherry Boone O'Neill

Dear Cherry:

Do you personally answer mail? I need some help in my recovery from anorexia. Actually, my problem is more bulimic than anorexic. I cannot control my appetite. It seems I have even lost the ability to know what a normal-sized meal is. If I eat until I am full, I have gone too far and I am faced with the terrible choice of discomfort and more pounds or falling back into throwing up and laxative usage. Is your appetite normal? If it is, how long did it take to stabilize? It seems like every time I eat it is a major ordeal in my life. I know I have no one to blame but myself. Will you write me a letter?

Dena R.
Anchorage, Alaska

Dear Dena:

As you can see, I do personally answer my mail, although it can be extremely challenging to keep up with the many who are facing your problem. You are definitely not alone in your quest to rid yourself of this illness. The question of appetite is very common among those with eating disorders and something with which I have had to deal in my own recovery. When our own natural digestive processes are short-circuited or abused, the natural consequences will always catch up with us. One of these is appetite, the signal which is transmitted from the brain alerting us to eat or to stop eating. After years of illness I found that my appetite was not a dependable indicator of what I really needed. It took the better part of a year for me to begin to once again rely on this feature of my body to tell me the truth. I don't know how many times I would turn to my husband, Dan, in frustration and ask, "Do you think I have eaten too much?" I honestly didn't know how to approach normal eating after years of abuse. It is a tremendous blessing to be surrounded by relatives or close friends who will help us to work through appropriate eating behavior when we can't fully trust ourselves. I might suggest that, if bingeing is a temptation for you, eat several small meals throughout the day rather than relying on one, two or three larger ones which may get you into trouble. If you are not totally full, there will be less chance that you will feel regret and attempt to purge yourself through vomiting or laxative abuse. If you have not done so already, think seriously about receiving some expert input in the area of eating disorders.

Cherry O'Neill

✗C✗C

Dear Cherry:

I am a junior in high school, I am five feet three in height and I weigh 95 pounds. Last week someone anonymously left your book in my locker. My locker partner swears it was not her and I believe her. I have had a problem with overeating and throwing up for some time but no one knows it but me. At least I thought nobody knew. Now I can't stand the thought of knowing that there are people looking at me as though I am a very sick person. I don't see myself as sick. I think people were cruel to put the book in my locker instead of talking to me. Please don't get the wrong idea because I think your book is very good but I know my problems are not as bad as yours were.

Stephanie J.
Northridge, Calif.

Dear Stephanie:

I am truly sorry that the circumstances in which you found my book caused you discomfort. I'll just bet your friends really care about you and, not knowing how to discuss the matter with you, simply dropped the anonymous "gift" into your locker for your review. You may not see yourself as sick—I know I didn't for a long, long time. But I have to be honest with you and tell you that overeating and vomiting (bulimia) can lead to extremely dangerous health consequences. You may not be as sick as I was, but you might be heading in that direction. Why don't you check into local resources available to you—I know there are good doctors and support groups in your area. There are varying degrees of any illness—wouldn't you go to a doctor for medication if a previously mild infection suddenly threatened to invade with full force? Even normal, healthy people occasionally have checkups, sick or not. Go ahead and schedule an appointment for evaluation and let the doctor diagnose your condition. Don't delay!

Cherry Boone O'Neill

Dear Cherry:

I know I have reached the point where I need help. I became anorexic in 1982 following my father's death. He committed suicide. He was a very moody person and he had terrible bouts of depression. I feel that I have been rejected. You might be thinking, well, she's just feeling sorry for herself, and I suppose that's true. Sometimes I feel very good about myself and very confident. At other times I feel down and depressed. It is when I'm depressed that I eat too much of the wrong things which gets me into trouble. Do you think I have a split personality? Did you ever feel like that when you were sick? My mom says I should write you a letter because even if you don't write to me it will make me feel better.

Susan G.
St. Louis, Mo.

Dear Susan:

It is very normal for us to experience some kind of grief reaction when we lose a loved one, particularly if it is one of our parents. I have spoken with other anorexic girls who have encountered the same tragedy in life. You may be encouraged to know that you have a headstart on beating your problem because if it began as recently as 1982, it may be corrected more easily than an illness of much longer duration. I find it very interesting that you are asking about the possibility of a split personality—this is almost exactly the question I put to my own psychiatrist in the midst of one particular therapy session. I thought that perhaps I was schizophrenic which seemed a frightening possibility. My doctor diagnosed my condition as a mild case of manic-depression or what some people have called "mood swing." For a period of time I was placed on lithium carbonate (a mineral salt available by prescription) which dramatically evened out my temperament. This allowed me to concentrate more effectively on the process of getting well. I was less compulsive and more even-tempered. I would highly recommend that you read the book *Mood Swing* by Dr. Ronald Fieve. But don't take my word for it—get a medical opinion on this matter, preferably from a psychotherapist who may be able to help bring your eating disorder under control.

Cherry O'Neill

✺C✺C

Dear Cherry O'Neill:

When you came to Australia I saw you on television. I tried to call the station but they would not give me your hotel telephone number. I purchased your book in hopes that I might learn more about my own problems. I suffer from the "slimmers' disease," as you have probably guessed. In some ways your story has helped me to better understand myself but some of the techniques you used to lose weight were previously unknown to me and I borrowed them. In some ways your book has actually made my problem worse. I wish you hadn't gone into certain details of your illness. I am writing to the publisher and he has promised to forward my letter to you.

Kathleen O.
Sydney, Australia

Dear Kathleen:

I received your letter last week which brought back memories of our trip to Australia. Although we were extremely busy with the media, we did have time to see your beautiful country and we hope to return again someday for a more relaxed vacation. Yours is the first letter I have received that states that weight loss techniques I mentioned in my book were borrowed by the reader. I must admit that, from the very beginning, I had some misgivings about just how much to share. Total honesty seemed like the only approach and I believe it has been this transparency which has given the story credibility. I truly regret that your condition may have been complicated by your newly acquired techniques, but ultimately, you must bear responsibility for your own decisions. This is part of growing up and getting well. I sincerely hope that you will find the help necessary to conquer your illness, such as professional psychotherapy, which I know is available in Australia. For a list of local resources, please write to my publisher, Dove Communications. Best wishes to you, Kathleen.

Cherry O'Neill

❧C❧C

Dear Cherry:

I am a recovered anorexic and am very thankful for what you are doing to help others who have been in our position. I know you are saving lives. I also had bulimia and, although I would like to say I am totally recovered, I cannot make that claim for the following reason. Every time there is a major holiday, such as Christmas, a birthday, Thanksgiving or other special occasions, I lose control and overeat. When it's all over I experience terrible guilt and regret and wonder how I could be so foolish. Can you honestly say you are never tempted? How do you handle Thanksgiving and Christmas which can be emotionally stressful and extremely tempting because of the emphasis on meals? I am a thirty-five-year-old housewife and mother of three children.

Heather Y.
Cleveland, Ohio

Dear Heather:

One of the basic keys in overcoming the temptations of bulimia is avoiding the *occasion* for temptation. Most of the time, this is relatively simple, however, as you have pointed out, holidays represent a special challenge. How clearly I remember Thanksgiving and Christmas when food was piled high and saying "no" became a near impossibility! Because you are a wife and mother I am going to assume that you have some control over the process of food preparation in your household. It would be wise to prepare yourself well in advance of holidays for the demands of special meals and food choices. You could avoid high calorie, rich foods which are a special temptation to bulimics and you may also attempt to prepare smaller portions. The time will come eventually when those trigger foods are no longer a threat to your willpower, but until then, you might as well lessen the tension of the holiday season. If your family is aware of your problem, they will undoubtedly understand your cautious approach to holiday food preparation. Limited exercise, meditation or other stress reducing techniques will also take the emotional edge off of those times during the year when we are particularly challenged in the area of weight control. I can honestly say I am no longer tempted to binge and purge and I know with careful planning and the support of your family, you will also be able to make that claim!

Cherry Boone O'Neill

꒳꒷꒳

Dear Cherry:

You are the only person I have to turn to for help. I'm not anorexic (at least I don't think I am) because I weigh 142 pounds. But I was up to 188 pounds. I feel terrible about being a "fat person." Only recently did I confess to my husband that I have been using diuretics and amphetamines, commercial diet capsules, laxatives—I even take No-Doz to stay awake. After all of this I am still fat. I feel exhausted and demoralized. None of the diet plans seem to work for me and I know I can't live with being overweight the rest of my life. My husband says I should see a doctor, but the question is, what kind? I have reached the point of desperation. Help!

Donna D.
Carson City, Nev.

Dear Donna:

You may not be anorexic by most definitions of the word, but the challenge you face may be no less formidable. You have obviously put yourself through much physical and psychological pain in order to lose 44 pounds. My recommendation would be that you do not think of yourself as a "fat person." This should not be your true identity. You may ask yourself the question, "Who would I be if I weighed exactly what I wanted to weigh?" If one's identity, or self-image, is that of being a "fat person" or a "thin person," then weight gain or loss automatically jeopardizes that person's security and mental health. Our self-image must be built on our inner qualities, not external appearances, contrary to what worldly values would seem to dictate. Self-image is the important concept here and I would suggest that you invest some personal energy into developing a positive one, preferably with professional assistance. It is good that you have confided in your husband, because you will need his support and feedback as you take on this challenge. I would urge you to level with your family doctor and seek his advice. Most doctors are happy to offer referrals to other professionals qualified in eating disorders and counseling. It is very possible that once you find out who the real Donna is, the weight problems may take care of themselves over a period of time.

Cherry

✕C✕C

Dear Cherry:

It has taken me years to admit that I have a problem. I know I must turn my life around, but so far it has been a losing battle. My fear is that I will put on weight and never be able to stop. As I'm sure you know by now, I am referring to anorexia nervosa. Everyone is telling me that I should get professional medical help by a qualified therapist. I feel quite strongly that since I developed the problem on my own, I should try to deal with it on my own. I like to think of myself as an independent person. I am a professional person in my early forties and not some disoriented kid who needs a counselor. I would simply like you to share with me some of what you learned in overcoming your problem. There must be certain keys to gaining control of your appetite and what kind of foods to eat or which ones to avoid. Also, if you have any reading material to suggest, I would be open to further research on the subject. I would appreciate any leads you can give me.

Charlotte S.
Trenton, N.J.

Dear Charlotte:

You may think of yourself as a mature person in mid-life, independent, educated and strong. Most anorexics, in fact, think of themselves as being disciplined and in control when ultimately, nothing could be further from the truth. I went through this myself. You are dealing with something that is bigger than you are. That is why you need help. Look at it this way—we all depend on each other to some degree. I'm sure that you would readily admit that you did not make your own shoes, design your watch or build your own car. It took others to provide you with these necessities in life. The same is true in the area of health care. We frequently need highly qualified, professional assistance. This does not mean we are weak, excessively dependent or out of control. In fact, asking for help when we need it is actually a sign of strength and maturity. By the way, if you've done any reading about eating disorders, you will find that family histories, relationships, biochemistry and other factors enter into this very complex equation which is why professional medical attention is warranted. I am enclosing a reading list which will answer most any question you have on diet and nutrition, but I would strongly urge you to locate a competent therapist as well.

Cherry

✖C✖C

Dear Mrs. O'Neill:

I am a student at _____ High School in Los Angeles not far from where you grew up. I have always been active in athletics, until recently, that is. I have had to drop out of all extracurricular activities because of my illness. I have the same thing you had. It all started last year when my coach urged me to lose a few extra pounds. He said I had the potential to be one of the best gymnasts he had ever coached. In attempting to go on to be the best, I have become the worst! Now I know I have no future in athletics and my dreams of competition are broken.

Jeannette E.
Los Angeles, Calif.

Dear Jeannette:

You are not the first nor will you be the last person who has written to me about excessive weight loss which began with a recommendation from a coach. The competition of athletics frequently tends to distort our values, particularly in the area of body image. Coaches, especially those directing younger students, could stand to be a lot more sensitive to the potential consequences of their suggestions. Rather than viewing your career in athletics as over and done, simply set a new goal and meet a new challenge, which is to conquer your illness and win big! The results will be far more than a trophy or a medal, as I'm sure you will agree. Just remember something from your gymnastic days—a positive mental attitude, persistence and patience with yourself will eventually bring you success.

Cherry Boone O'Neill

✂✂

Dear Cherry:

I tried to write you once before, but your letter came back because it was the wrong address. Then I wrote to your father's office and his secretary gave me your address. I have always been a fan of the Pat Boone family. I watched your television specials and have most of the records. My mom even has some of your dad's old 45 RPM records in her collection. I always thought of you Boones as the perfect family—then I read your story in *Starving for Attention* and was very surprised about how you lied and deceived people. Does this mean you were a hypocrite before? I hope this doesn't offend you, but I always looked up to you, even more than the other Boone girls. Why did you feel you had to deceive people?

J. M. Miller
Orlando, Fla.

Dear J.M.:

You are correct in your observation of my earlier inconsistencies. I suppose you can say that one of my problems was the fact that I thought we were supposed to be the perfect family. I saw myself as the exception and therefore felt I should hide my flaws and inadequacies. While I regret lying and deception, I have now come to recognize that I was truly ill. I was not fully responsible for many of my actions. The real pressure came in knowing I was an example, a role model, for so many young people. This made me feel terrible when I knew my life was really complicated with severe problems. I felt I had to put the best face on a bad situation for the sake of others. This, by the way, is true with many of the celebrities I have known in the show business world. I have come to realize, however, that human beings are fallible and families all have their problems. Ours is no exception. I would urge you to take your eyes off of human "idols"—you are sure to be disappointed sooner or later. Also, it is important to understand that we must all make our own decisions and cannot lay them at the feet of another.

Cherry O'Neill

❧❦❧

Dear Cherry O'Neill:

I am writing to you as a last resort. We are truly desperate because our eighteen-year-old daughter, Sheila, is in the hospital for the third time in two years with a relapse of anorexia nervosa. She refuses to eat so she is being fed intravenously. Believe it or not, she even exercises in her hospital bed! She was a straight A student all through junior high and high school until this year. She was out of school so many days with her illness that her teachers told her she would have to repeat her classes. This made matters even worse. She has always been a perfectionist. The amazing thing is she says she looks fat and she only weighs 85 pounds. Her doctor says Sheila could die if this continues. Her case sometimes seems hopeless. Has she gone too far? When you were hospitalized, what was your weight and what was the turning point for you in recovery?

Mr. and Mrs. J. Walker
Atlanta, Ga.

Dear Mr. and Mrs. Walker:

I was hospitalized at 80 pounds—perhaps even a little less. Like Sheila, I found ways of deceiving my nursing staff by not eating and exercising in my room during their meal breaks. Desperation is a tremendous motivator. Although I left the hospital heavier and seemingly healthier, it was a temporary solution, for me, because I was only dealing with the symptoms and not underlying, root causes. Dealing with the external only is like putting Band-Aids on the slashed wrists of a victim of a suicide attempt. The turning point in my life came when I sought psychotherapy for my anorexia and bulimia. Because I do not know Sheila's condition, I cannot judge if she has "gone too far." I will tell you this—it is amazing how much suffering and abuse the human body can endure this side of death. At this point, doctors undoubtedly see their job as one of simply saving her life, after which time weight will be *gradually* gained to a point where she will be able to rationally respond to professional therapy. All of this, of course, takes time. Be patient and never give up hope! My thoughts and prayers are with you.

Cherry Boone O'Neill

Dear Mrs. O'Neill:

I just finished reading your book. I couldn't put it down! I saw myself on every page, and cried all the way through. I no longer feel like a freak or that I'm all alone because now I know you and many others have gone through the same thing. I wish I could say I have recovered but I'm afraid I haven't even taken the first step in that direction. Where can I turn for help? I am sixteen and I am thinking about talking to my school counselor.

Judy R.
Burbank, Calif.

Dear Judy:

Your letter just arrived today and because I believe you're in a critical and highly motivated phase of your life, I am getting this note right out to you. Act on your emotional response to my story. Let the seriousness of your condition and the hopeful possibilities of recovery guide you toward competent counseling. Not only should you speak with your school counselor, but you should seriously consider sharing with family members or friends (those you can truly trust) so you may build a support group around yourself. Be prepared for setbacks and disappointments along the way— it would not be fair of me to ignore this warning because I know how they affected me. But don't let them derail you from your forceful movement toward health! Best wishes to you, Judy.

Cherry Boone O'Neill

P.S. You may not realize it, but you have indeed taken that first step toward recovery—you reached outside of yourself for help by writing to me. Now move on to step #2!

＊C＊C

Dear Cherry O'Neill:

I hope this letter reaches you and that somehow you will find the time to reply to me. Your book has offered me hope that someday I may get well. I have been suffering from anorexia nervosa and bulimia for more than four years. Now I cannot stop losing weight. I'm afraid if even one ounce is added to my body, I will not be able to stop gaining. I have nightmares about being fat. This morning I watched your interview on The 700 Club and I knew I had to write to you. You know so much about my problem. Will you counsel me? I really want to get well but I don't know where to begin. Please write soon!

L. L. Thompson
Pittsburgh, Pa.

P.S. I'm 19 years old and now weigh 97 pounds.

Dear L. Thompson:

One of the greatest fears of an anorexic or bulimic is that they will gain weight in the recovery process and never stop adding pounds. I think this was my own greatest fear as I faced getting well. But let me share something with you. When you really stop to think about how many of the things we fear truly come to pass, it is very few—give it some consideration. The same is true of weight gain. Certainly, recovery will necessitate putting on some weight but it can and should be done gradually. You will learn how to maintain at a healthy level. Your weight will not increase uncontroll-ably. Your anxieties are exaggerated. This is what an eating disorder does—it distorts our perceptions. It is a kind of terror which others around you will not understand which is why you should see a competent, qualified therapist. I cannot counsel you or specifically advise you—that is for the experts. But I can give you hope and extend encouragement. I am pulling for you!

Cherry

ℵℂℵℂ

Dear Cherry:

I am writing to you about my sister, Jeanne, who has anorexia nervosa. She is seventeen and I am fourteen. We also have a younger brother. We are all upset about Jeanne's condition. Our whole family is upset. We saw you on television. Can you help us? My parents are divorced and Jeanne took it hardest of all. Is this her problem? She fixes all the food in the family. She can make a perfect dinner, but she never eats it. She just watches us eat. She is always fighting with us. She is in a bad mood most of the time. She won't listen to us. Do you think she would listen to you? Could you write a letter? My mom says you will never write because you are famous and because you are too busy.

Theresa M.
Houston, Tex.

Dear Theresa:

Your sister may have borne grief over your parents' divorce from which she has been unable to recover. It is not unusual for an anorexic to have difficulty in resolving normal grief feelings. You also mentioned her mood. This can be an extremely important factor in your sister's health problem. She may be experiencing depression. You may want to look that word up in the dictionary or in a medical book to see exactly what the clinical definition is. It is frequently beyond our ability to control and can be extremely damaging in many areas of our lives. Please don't blame her for being depressed. What she needs now, more than ever, is understanding and love even though it is very difficult to deal with her on a day-to-day basis. If Jeanne would take my advice, I would direct her toward expert help in the area of eating disorders. But this must ultimately be her decision, not yours or mine. And one more thing, Theresa. Please look up the word *empathy* and possibly *compassion*. These may be important skills for you to learn if you really want to help your sister decide to get well.

Cherry Boone O'Neill

⚜

Dear Cherry:

I need some advice and because you are the only person I know who has recovered from anorexia and bulimia, I am writing in hopes you will respond. My roommate and I are nursing students at UCLA. Last week I caught Sharon vomiting after dinner. At first she denied it, then claimed she was ill. Since that time I have found other evidence that she is bulimic. Last year I read your book, *Starving for Attention*, and found it a fascinating study in illness and recovery. I have thought about giving it to Sharon, but I'm afraid to confront her. I am also afraid to allow her to continue with her self-destructiveness. The ironic thing is that she has been involved in treating anorexics at the hospital and has helped many girls to recover. Should I give her your book or just be supportive?

J. D.
Van Nuys, Calif.

Dear J. D.:

Sharon, though she is apparently exhibiting symptoms of bulimia, may be better prepared to deal with anorexics or bulimics at the hospital than those who have never experienced these disorders. She can empathize with them and perhaps touch them in ways that others can't. On the other hand, it is important that she receive treatment, and you may be the key. The primary question regards the durability of your friendship. You may have to risk confrontation. Perhaps leaving my book, or some other reading material on eating disorders where she may find it would be a good place to begin. If she's truly interested, as I guess she will be, the material will be read. Among those who are stricken with eating disorders, there is quite a high percentage of achievers, professional people, and those, like nurses, who are performance-oriented. As the subject evolves naturally, you may suggest that she go to a staff physician for advice—there should be no shortage of experts where she works! Good luck.

Cherry Boone O'Neill

P.S. There are a number of support groups for victims of eating disorders in your area. Perhaps you could offer to go along for moral support. Not only would she benefit from others with her condition, she would boost her self-esteem as she observes her shared experience and expertise helping other members.

❧❧

Dear Cherry:

I am writing to you out of desperation and confusion. After reading your book on anorexia, I knew I could get well too. I know you come from a very committed Christian family, so I hope you can answer my question. We go to a nondenominational church which believes in the spiritual gift of healing. My pastor and a visiting evangelist prayed for me last Sunday evening. They told me to simply "claim my healing" and believe that God would make me better. (I've been suffering from anorexia nervosa since I was thirteen. I am now sixteen and also have bulimia.) In your book you said people prayed for you. You also said professional help was important. My pastor says I should not go to a worldly doctor but just believe God. I do believe in God, but I don't feel any different after being prayed for. Do I lack faith? Should I go to a doctor even though my parents don't want me to? They say I should submit to our church teaching (and to them!). I'm scared and I need an answer right away.

Janet W.
Indianapolis, Ind.

Dear Janet:

As a Christian, I believe that God is certainly able to heal. I know of some specific cases where miracles would seem to be the only explanation for recovery from an illness or injury. However, I know of no such cases involving anorexia or bulimia. I'm not prepared to say they have not happened, however, prudence would seem to dictate that we take advantage of any and all areas of assistance. I would venture to say that even your pastor goes to a physician on occasion, even if only for a checkup. My own doctor, Ray Vath, M.D., has stated that those with strong religious faith seem to have a better prognosis for recovery. I believe God has given great gifts of wisdom within the medical community and has allowed man to progress in understanding and learning toward great accomplishments, including the treatment of all kinds of diseases and disorders. By the way, I don't believe a doctor must be religious in order to have benefited by the fruits of medical advancement. Strong personal faith is not a prerequisite to expert medical credentials. In my own case, as I have stated before, I believe that God guided me to the kind of therapy that I needed to recover. I don't interpret this to be any less a miracle than a more obvious physical healing. Diplomacy is the key, here, Janet. I would attempt to strike a balance while realizing that the severity of your situation may call for immediate diagnosis by a qualified medical doctor. Perhaps there are others in your church who would value expert medical guidance for their own concerns who could share your thoughts with your pastor and parents. You will probably discover that it's not a matter of lack of faith on your part, but a lack of true understanding of your health situation on theirs. My prayers are with you.

Cherry

❧❦❧

Dear Cherry Boone O'Neill:

For the first time in my life I am reaching out to someone with my problem, which *was* your problem, anorexia nervosa. I am thirty-one years old, my husband is in the oil business and we have everything we have ever wanted. I have two beautiful children and I know that people say that we are the perfect family. Our social circle includes well-known celebrities, business people and politicians, both state and federal. I have always felt the pressure to be the perfect hostess/wife which also means being slim and beautiful. What began as a sensible diet degenerated into a desperate battle with anorexia and bulimia. When I am home alone, I can't stop crying. I hate myself and yet I cannot stop eating and purging. I am addicted to laxatives and I know this can't be good for my body. If I seek help, my secret will be known and I don't know if I am ready to risk that. I would be willing to fly to Seattle to talk to you, if you have time. I feel I am ready to make some decisions, but I need good advice. Thank you for reading this letter.

Mrs. T. B.
Fort Worth, Tex.

P.S. I have a six-year-old daughter and already I see that she is a perfectionist. Is it possible she could become anorexic at this age? Could she be picking up some of my bad habits?

Dear Mrs. B.:

I understand your position more than you may think. I, too, occupied a very visible social role, but the time came when tough choices had to be made. Don't let your pride stand between you and your health. I came to the conclusion that it is simply not worth it. There are few who can extricate themselves from the eating/purging cycle without some type of outside help and I would urge you to seek it while at the same time to point out that I do not feel qualified to chart a specific course of action beyond recommending medical intervention. Also, the sooner you seek help, the sooner you will be able to move in a healthier direction which will ultimately benefit your daughter. For better or worse, we are the first and most powerful teachers of our children. Modeling is an extraordinary behavioral influence and your daughter may well be affected by your disorder. But as a word of encouragement, she is also young and will be positively impressed by your recovery process. The sooner the better!

Cherry Boone O'Neill

P.S. You will be amazed to discover that as you open up to

your peers regarding areas of challenge in your life, they will tend to divulge their own struggles. Your gradual candidness may end up saving other lives, as well as your own.

✁✁

Dear Ms. O'Neill:

Teri and I have lived together for two years and we hoped to be married after my graduation from the University of Washington this coming Spring. In the past year she suddenly developed what appears to be anorexia nervosa. She claims she is not vomiting or abusing laxatives but I honestly don't know if she is telling me the truth. She is despondent and has even talked about suicide. I am walking on pins and needles. When she gains two or three pounds, I tell her she looks great and she goes into a depression. She says this means she has put on weight and she fears losing control. She knows I wouldn't mind if she were overweight but she says she can't live with herself unless she can be slim. She has become increasingly irritable and it seems anything I say, even if it is complimentary, is taken as criticism or as an insult. She is hypersensitive to any mention of food (she refuses to eat in front of me, but she will eat in secret) or weight. I think I might be living with a life-and-death situation. She has read your book and would probably read a letter if you have time to send one. I hope this is not a great inconvenience for you, but I'm sure you will understand the intensity of the situation.

R. R. Marshall
Bellevue, Wash.

Dear R.:

The symptoms sound all too familiar. If you and Teri are headed toward marriage, it will be vitally important that you honestly share the situation with one another in advance and even make headway toward healing. Otherwise, the conflict you may be experiencing now will only worsen with time and your marriage may fall prey to severe buffeting even before it has a chance to solidify. Perhaps you could seek referrals from the University of Washington Hospital medical staff (I know they are first-rate!) for therapy or other experts. Teri will continue to be extremely sensitive, for a while, to the areas of concern you have pointed out in your letter. Just remember, she is even more aware of them than you and probably does not need to have them pointed out. Your role is to be as accepting and supportive as you can, urging her toward more full disclosure and ultimately professional help. By the way, you mentioned depression. Mood disorders are frequently a significant part of the disorder. Just one more reason to get a good doctor on this case!

Cherry O'Neill

ᕦᏟᕦᏟ

Dear Cherry:

You don't know me but I have followed your father's career and your family's lives for many years. I went to school with your parents in Nashville but lost touch with them years ago. I suppose I have been one of your father's biggest fans! Debby's song, "You Light Up My Life" is my daughter's favorite. Kimberly is now twenty-one years old and has fallen victim to the "dieters' disease." I was very surprised to learn that you suffered from the same illness which you talked about on the Merv Griffin Show. We are a good Christian family with a deep faith in God and we have been praying for two years that she will recover. Her father and I are becoming very worried as her weight has dropped below 92 pounds. Is psychiatric help the only way of dealing with this problem? Is heavy laxative use a symptom of this illness? Any help you can give us would be greatly appreciated!

Ann Marie F.
Memphis, Tenn.

Dear Ann Marie:

It sounds to me as though you have been keeping up with Boone family news! Yes, as you heard, I had the "dieters' disease" or anorexia nervosa. Heavy laxative use could indicate bulimia, a syndrome involving bingeing and purging. You may want to do some reading up on the subjects. I know people may tire of me saying that medical help, psychotherapy if possible, is the best form of treatment—but it's true. If I am reading between the lines correctly, I sense a hesitancy on your part to get this kind of help. Many people, particularly Christians, feel that they are admitting failure or a weakened faith by seeking the counsel of a psychiatrist, but nothing could be further from the truth. It is just as legitimate to treat the mind, emotions and their problems as it is to undergo heart surgery. I believe it is becoming increasingly "okay" to seek such help in Christian circles. Certainly, if we don't, our witness will be further impaired as the consequences of serious illness become more evident. Attempt to find a doctor who has a good track record in the area of eating disorders. God bless you and your family.

Cherry O'Neill

Dear Cherry:

I would be surprised if you remember who we are because so many people must be contacting you about your illness and recovery. My husband called your husband about a month ago because he was at the end of his rope as far as my illness is concerned. I have been anorexic for about five years and things have gotten so bad that our marriage has been threatened. Anyway, your husband was very encouraging to Tom, and he now sees a lot of hope for us if we would move away from San Jose (he has contacted a doctor in Los Angeles). I must confess that I am afraid. I vacillate between wanting to hang on to my anorexia and wanting to get well, and I know I don't want to leave this area where my parents live. We have always been a very close family. My husband and I have both read your story and heard you on a radio talk show. That is when Tom decided to track down your husband, Dan. I feel weak, confused and unable to make any decisions. I could sure use some guidance from one who has been there.

Florence R.
San Jose, Calif.

Dear Florence:

Your situation sounds much like mine was in 1977. I also was sick, weak, confused and, frankly, a little terrified at the prospects of leaving home. I couldn't believe I was actually going to see a psychiatrist—after all, I knew I was sick but I didn't think I was crazy! Then I reached the point where I simply had to trust the affirmative action that Dan was taking. I would urge you to do the same. In some ways you may look at this as an adventure and you always have the mail, telephones and, resources permitting, air travel to keep you in touch with your family. It could well be that you need

95

to disengage a bit from your loved ones to develop your own identity and to seek new life in a new place, at least for a while. (By the way, I do remember your situation which Dan reported to me when your husband called him at the office.) Consider yourself fortunate to have a caring husband and the soon-coming support of a good physician.

Cherry Boone O'Neill

※C※C

Dear Mrs. O'Neill:

I am a high school student in a private girls' school in Dallas. I read your story in *People* magazine. I loved the pictures! I bought your book, *Starving for Attention,* and finished it in two days. I am sending it to you to sign—I hope you don't mind! You went through a lot, but I'm glad to hear you are recovered. I am now doing a report on anorexia nervosa. Is anorexia a physical problem or a mental problem? How long did it take you to recover? And why do you think people do things like this when it is so dangerous to their health?

Talia J.
Dallas, Tex.

Dear Talia:

Here is your autographed book and a brief note. I am also including a reading list to help you with your report on anorexia nervosa. To answer your question briefly, anorexia is both a mental and a physical problem. The obvious symptoms are physical and in themselves can cause tremendous problems and even threaten life. But the underlying causes are psychological in nature, creating an extremely complex disorder which may have many contributing factors.

My recovery took place over about a year's time, for the most part, but I struggled with certain symptoms for even longer. It is not uncommon for a person to take years—the average is three to five—to conquer this illness. If I knew the answer to why anorexics and people with other eating disorders engaged in self-destructive activity, I would be a medical genius, which I certainly am not. Almost all anorexics are perfectionists with low self-esteem. In time, low self-esteem may develop into depression and self-hatred. If you hate yourself, self-destructive behavior is a logical outgrowth. We don't know all of the reasons but more answers are emerging as research continues.

Cherry O'Neill

ꝲ℃ꝲ℃

Dear Cherry:

Hi again! I want to thank you for taking the time to write to me. I'm doing much better now and have been in therapy for about four months. My parents are even coming with me now although at first they said it was my problem and refused to participate. I'm still thin—96 pounds—but I feel much better. I know I'm going to make it, thanks to you and to my doctor. I am taking your advice and overcoming my own selfishness and depression by helping others. I would like to start a support group for girls who have anorexia nervosa. By helping them, I know I can also help myself. Would you come and speak to our group? My doctor says he is glad I want to help others in my condition, but he thinks it may be a little too soon, what do you think? Please write soon.

Judith A.
Miami, Fla.

Dear Judith:

I am so glad to hear you are making progress in recovering from your illness. Yes, you are still thin, but at 96 pounds you are obviously making headway and it's best to put on weight slowly. Don't try to move too quickly or take on too many new things in your life at this point. You can grow into that—remember, recovery is a process. Support groups are good and I would recommend one for you, however, I would be careful of directing one. I agree with your doctor—wait a while and gain some experience and confidence first. You may be interested to know that some of the best counselors and therapists I know have, at one time in their lives, experienced this disorder which gives them an advantage in dealing with it in the lives of others. But take your time!

Cherry Boone O'Neill

)C)C

Dear Cherry:

I don't know where else to go so I'm writing to you. I am a prisoner in my own home. I am twenty-two years old and my parents dominate me completely. They say I am too sick to live by myself because I am suffering from anorexia nervosa and bulimia. They are always checking up on me even to the point of going through my purse and accompanying me to the bathroom. It is so humiliating. My mother is jealous because she cannot control her weight. They want me to go to a doctor but it must be the one that *they* choose. I don't see any hope of things improving but if you have any ideas, please jot them down and drop them in the mail. Even though I am an adult I am made to feel like a child. How did your parents deal with your illness? I read your book but I'm sure there is more to the story.

Janet S.
Columbus, Ohio

Dear Janet:

It is not difficult to understand why caring parents would make every effort, even though those measures may be inappropriate at times, to deal with a daughter's illness. This is especially true with an eating disorder which seems so frightening, complex and persistent. I would suggest, however, that at twenty-two years of age you may be permitting and even perpetuating their behavior—we are only dominated to the extent we allow it, in many cases. Let's face it, there is a certain amount of security being at home and being told what to do even though the situation may be most unpleasant. Their detective techniques in dealing with some of your symptoms are not unlike the ones I experienced in my own home, even from my own husband in the early months of our marriage. The problem here is that it oftentimes tends to make one even more deceptive and introverted. Overall, it is counterproductive. Perhaps you could incorporate some diplomacy in your situation by requesting that they give you more personal space while you promise to go ahead and see the doctor of their choice. If he's a qualified expert, he will recognize the family dynamics involved and deal with them or refer you to another doctor. At first, my own family and husband attempted to be directive and even coercive in their longing to see me recover. But it became apparent after a few sessions with my therapist that I was the one that would ultimately have to choose life over death, health over sickness. To be quite honest, there was not a lot more to the story than you read in the book. It was painful to recount my story but I sincerely trust it will continue to help others who are in this predicament. I notice you did not mention a desire on your part to recover—this must be your first order of business. If you do want to get well there are creative possibilities that can be worked out in your family with the advice of a competent physician. There are anorexics, however, who do not wish to give up their illness for a variety of reasons. You may want to think this over carefully before making the most important decision of your life—I hope you choose to embark upon a journey toward life.

Cherry Boone O'Neill

Dear Cherry:

You may not remember our conversation but you spoke with me after a concert your family did at a state fair here in Ohio. My name is Gretchen and you signed a record album for me at the end of your last concert. That was in 1976. Since that time I have battled with anorexia nervosa on and off. I have been hospitalized four times but it never seems to be a lasting solution for me. I have suffered from severe depression which makes each day seem like an eternity for me. It's hard for me to believe that I could get well. I still live at home with my father even though I am twenty-three years old. (My mother died in 1977 of cancer.) Any words of encouragement you may have for me would be very much appreciated.

Gretchen D.
Cincinnati, Ohio

Dear Gretchen:

Yes, I do remember the concert we did in Ohio. To be honest, I don't remember signing an album, but I suppose that is understandable since we frequently were asked for autographs after our performances. Regarding your current condition, I would encourage you to read some of the latest material which indicates that mood disorders, particularly depression, have a lot to do with anorexia nervosa and bulimia (reading list enclosed). Although I did not recognize it as depression, that was one of the problems I faced during my illness and, even now, I must keep close tabs on this particular area of my life. Psychotherapy coupled with appropriate medication under the careful supervision of a qualified physician could be just the answer for you, but I would strongly emphasize that you seek some kind of competent, professional help. Though you didn't relate it specifically to your anorexia, grief over the loss of a loved one, if left unresolved, may be a contributing factor which you may want to consider. Again, this could be part of your treatment program with a doctor. I certainly wish you every blessing as you pursue good health—remember, it will take time and patience.

Cherry

✕C✕C

Dear Cherry Boone O'Neill:

I am not writing to ask for anything, not even a reply. I am just saying "thank you" for the wonderful work you are doing in helping victims of the self-starvation disease. I am a grandmother with four children and seven grandchildren, all of them very healthy. I read about your story in our diocesan (Catholic) newspaper and found it interesting that you and Dan now work with an organization helping the poor in other parts of the world. Isn't it just like God to take you from illness and suffering to becoming a great blessing to many, both here and in other countries. Can you tell me more about this organization? I think I heard somewhere that your parents are involved with this work also. Thank you again for being a blessing to so many!

Mrs. Wilda C.
Philadelphia, Pa.

Dear Wilda:

Thank you for your comments regarding the work we are doing. In 1979, my husband, Dan, and my parents started Mercy Corps International. It is a nonprofit, humanitarian relief and development organization based in Seattle and Portland. Mercy Corps works with the homeless, the hungry and other hurting people in troubled spots around the world. Dan is chairman of the board of this organization and finds the work tremendously rewarding (for further information, write to Mercy Corps International, 115 N 85th Street, Suite 102, Seattle, WA 98103). Dan and I found that one of the ways to put our own problems in perspective is to reach out to others who are in desperate need. After years of focusing on my own starvation, once my healing process began I was able to help reach out to others through this new vehicle. I frequently recommend that those with eating disorders find ways of helping or touching those in need in some meaningful way, which could include volunteer work or donating to a charitable cause. The obvious irony of anorexia and bulimia in America is that in the midst of great material wealth, there are many literally starving to death around us. I have found it uplifting to offer assistance and hope to those who are desperately poor and, through no fault of their own, are suffering from hunger or other types of deprivation.

Cherry Boone O'Neill

⚜

Dear Cherry:

I come from a family with a history of weight problems. I am the only thin one in our family and it is because I have disciplined myself through exercise and dieting. I am determined that I will never be fat even if I must resort to continued use of laxatives and vomiting. My father has become suspicious of my weight control and took me to a doctor for a physical and then another visit a month later. To my father's surprise Dr. Cooperman said that I am the healthiest one in the family and that it would do the others a lot of good to follow my example in controlling my weight. I am 101 pounds although I have been down to 98. Deep down this bothers me because I know I have deceived my family and even my doctor. If I can deceive even my doctor, how can he help me? Are there other ways besides the use of laxatives and purging to keep my weight where it is?

Diane F.
Des Moines, Iowa

Dear Diane:

You are apparently in a situation where inherited family characteristics are not to your liking. You can never run away from those genetic blueprints—I guess you know that. I would suggest that you attempt to deal with this reality instead of attempting to do the impossible. The "set point" theory of body weight is based on the assumption that we all have a specific level which is ideal and from which we can never drift beyond certain perimeters for any length of time without jeopardizing our health. This does not mean that you should not attempt to develop certain appropriate disciplines such as nutritious eating and exercise. Your doctor may be able to give you some bearing on an approach to weight control that is best suited for you personally. And regarding your doctor, remember he is only human and can only work with the facts he receives. If you are withholding information, he will be unable to deal with your condition effectively. I would urge you to take that big step and risk sharing some details, facts and figures with him. Ultimately, you will be relieved and will begin to "turn the corner." By the way, I would be remiss if I failed to warn you that laxative abuse and self-induced vomiting can be extremely hazardous to your health.

Cherry

✕✕

Dear Mrs. O'Neill:

I hope I am not intruding into your life by writing to you but I am just about at my wits' end. My oldest daughter, Carrie, who is fifteen, is seeing a therapist for anorexia. This has been a tremendous strain on the family both emotionally and financially. Now my other daughter, Christine, who is thirteen, refuses to eat and has lost five pounds. I can't believe this is happening in a society of plenty. I can't believe it is happening in our family, and with both of our daughters. Is there something wrong with our family? Is this going around in the schools? My husband says this is a phase and that the girls will grow out of it as they get older. I believe we should not treat this illness lightly as I have heard that it has a 15 percent mortality rate. I hope you are able to find the time to give me a reply.

Mrs. T. E. Lowry
Hartford, Conn.

Dear Mrs. Lowry:

Your letter is not the first I have received where more than one member of a family is suffering from anorexia. The financial and emotional stress, I know, can be tremendous. Healing in itself can be stressful, as you may know, but the end results are worth the challenge. Don't presume that you have a bad family—this problem develops in the *best* of families. In some schools around the country anorexic and, especially, bulimic behaviors are epidemic. There seems to be a certain fascination with eating disorders that can lead to experimentation and playing with fire. It is estimated by some authorities that one to one and a half percent of American women will experience anorexia some time in their lives. Ten to twenty percent will become bulimic at some time in their lives. It is true that many will recover spontaneously, but it is important that you seek professional treatment as early as possible when symptoms show up. Please convey my greetings to Carrie and to Christine—I wish them well.

Cherry O'Neill

✗C ✗C

Dear Mr. and Mrs. O'Neill:

I read your book with great interest and I have highly recommended it to others. I have never seen such a candid, open confession of a problem which most people seek to keep "under wraps." I was particularly intrigued with the comparison that was made between your conversion to Catholicism and the process of healing. I am sure you could write another entire book on it, but do you think it would be possible to explain a bit further? I suppose you could call me a lapsed Catholic but lately I have given some consideration to returning to the church.

Doug C.
Mission Viejo, Calif.

Dear Doug:
We have received quite a number of letters on this subject. Dan has been asked to write a book on our conversion process and I believe he will probably give it some very serious consideration. Essentially, I was comparing our conversion to my healing in that both took place over a long period of time. It is important for people to realize that Christianity and healing are not one-time experiences but progressions. We compare conversion and healing to a journey or pilgrimage. By the way, we know a number of nonpracticing Catholics who are moving back toward new commitments to their faith. We certainly wish you the best as you seek your own path back to the church. God bless!

Cherry O'Neill

✼C✼C

Dear Cherry O'Neill:
This may come as a surprise to you but I'm a registered nurse working in a very well-known hospital here in New York City and I am also a victim of bulimia. As a high school student I became anorexic for approximately a year and one

half but recovered spontaneously. It was during that time that I became interested in nursing. I am an expert on the damage bulimic activity can cause and yet I cannot seem to break the habit. I feel like an addict—at least a slave to habit. While some of my co-workers are abusing prescription drugs from the hospital pharmacy (you wouldn't believe how much it happens), I am bingeing then ridding myself of what I have eaten. I read your book which I found here in the hospital library and I hope you don't mind me addressing some questions to you. Were you truly bulimic? If so, how did you break the cycle of habitual bingeing and purging? I know I can't continue like this but I also can't seem to control myself.

Atida D., RN
New York, N. Y.

Dear Atida:

It is not a real surprise to me that a person in the medical field (or any competitive, pressured field such as yours) should fall victim to an eating disorder. There are special challenges and stresses in your line of work which could perhaps contribute to such a problem. You obviously need no explanations from me regarding the consequences of bingeing and purging. I was, by definition, bulimic during the latter phase of my own battle with anorexia nervosa. Like you, I felt hopelessly addicted to a behavior pattern which medical expertise is only now coming to grips with in more detail. It has been suggested by some researchers that bingeing and purging are actually addicting because of biochemical changes which take place during the process. This may account for the inability of many to shake the habit. But there are ways out, and therapy is one of them. Some of the most recent advances in medication for depression have had a strong impact on bulimic activity. Let me suggest that you read

New Hope for Binge Eaters by Harrison G. Pope, Jr., and James T. Hudson (Harper and Row, 1984). Some of the material is quite technical but nothing a registered nurse could not fathom. You will find some intriguing comments on the causes of bulimia, treatment, the use of antidepressants and other helpful information. Don't forget to seek help and support from among your professional peers.

Cherry Boone O'Neill

✖C✖C

Dear Cherry:

I read the *Guidepost's* article on your rcovery from anorexia nervosa. It was a beautiful story. Can you tell me more about the role your faith played in getting well? Do you think it is a sin to have anorexia nervosa? Is there anywhere in the Bible where it talks about eating problems?

Jill H.
Nashville, Tenn.

Dear Jill:

Your letter was short but your questions are big! Yes, faith played an important role in my recovery. I know my doctor will attest to this and generally believes that those of strong religious faith have a better prognosis for recovery. Judgments as to whether certain actions or decisions are sinful is not as easy to answer since there seem to be many gray areas in life, particularly when illness is involved. I personally believe that once behavior moves into illness sin is a poor concept to use in dealing with the situation. If something is truly beyond our control, as I believe my own illness became, sin becomes a highly questionable moral description. Biblically speaking, you probably won't find anything about anorexia or bulimia mentioned; however, it is intriguing to note that man's fall centered around the tasting of forbidden fruit. It was through eating and disobedience that man fell, but it is also through eating that man experiences new life in the eucharist or communion. I find this development very interesting and I have derived great comfort through the years from this model of redemption which the church offers to us.

Cherry

⚮C⚮C

Dear Cherry:

I have been caught in a cycle of anorexia and bulimia for more than five years. This year I dropped out of college because my weakened condition would not allow me to study and hold a job. I feel like a failure, and on top of everything else, I feel guilty about hiding my problems from even my closest of friends. I can't go on leading a secretive life of hiding and yet I don't have the strength to come out of the closet, so to speak. I am so depressed I have considered suicide. I know life is not worth living if it goes on like this. I am open to any ideas you may have but I will understand if you don't have time to write.

Dorothy D.
Tulsa, Okla.

Dear Dorothy:

You are reaching out at a critical point in your life and this is a very important beginning. One of the reasons you feel like a failure is because failure is the inevitable consequence of being a perfectionist. No one can attain perfection. It is also not unusual for those with eating disorders to hide their problems from those around them. You say you don't have the strength to come out of the closet, but at least you've cracked the door just a bit by sharing your problem with me. Take that next step which is a little closer to truly confronting the reality of your condition. Depression is also common and I would speculate that if this area of your life is addressed through therapy and medication under the care of a qualified physician, the rest may come much easier for you. By the way, regarding college, don't feel alone. I left after two and a half years and I found that it was not the end of the world. And remember—it's never too late to go back!

Cherry O'Neill

Dear Cherry Boone O'Neill:

I am writing to you because I am starting to feel bad about my weight. I am sixteen years old, a better than average student and I weigh 135 pounds. By the way, I am five feet six inches tall. I am very uncomfortable with my weight which I feel is above what it should be. My boyfriend recently broke up with me, and even though he didn't say it, I am wondering if he thinks I'm overweight. My mom is 139 pounds and she thinks she is overweight too. I think I am starting to feel desperate about this. I tried running but I gave up in defeat. I wish I could have anorexia nervosa for about a month. I know you also felt fat when you were 140 pounds and in high school. Do you have any ideas for me?

Cynthia F.
Gibsonia, Pa.

Dear Cynthia:

Given the dimensions you wrote in your letter, I hardly feel you are "fat." I think there are a number of things that have contributed to your fears of obesity—your mother's concern with her own weight, your own apprehension at battling with the bulges like she has as you grow older, approval from your peers and probably a lot of what I consider to be unrealistic and unfair input from the media and the advertising world. Over the last twenty years, women who are not thin as a rail are made to feel uncomfortable with their body images through a constant bombardment of advertising and fashion trends, probably beginning about the time of Twiggy. This is very unfortunate because many impressionable people have been intimidated by sophisticated advertising into thinking they are second class citizens because of their weight. This has become such a problem that a recent survey of over 33,000 women by *Glamour Magazine* indicated that 75 percent of women think they are overweight! Obviously, not all of those women are overweight, and I'm sure you may fit into this category. In fact, 80 pecent of these women felt they had to be slim in order to be attractive to men. Another major factor in the survey showed that mothers transmitted unhappiness with their own bodies to their daughters. There are other factors involved in this poll, but I think you get the picture. You are worrying needlessly. I suggest that you attempt moderate exercise (I try to swim one hour a day, five days a week), design a healthy diet and develop friends who care about *who* you are, not what you look like. I hope this gives you food for thought!

Cherry Boone O'Neill

⚡C⚡C

Dear Mrs. O'Neill:

I am writing this letter hoping there is some small chance you may be able to personally answer it. I am hoping that you and maybe your husband can give me some feedback or some help. My wife is a semiprofessional dancer and aerobics instructor at a local health club. I am deeply involved in amateur athletics as a distance runner with a very good record. We have been married almost three years but the way things are going, divorce is a real possibility. I moved out last week. Shirley is anorexic and bulimic. In recent months, she has lost so much weight that she has not been able to work and she will rarely take my advice even though she acknowledges the fact that I know a fair amount about fitness and nutrition. (I read your book about a year ago, but I put off writing until now, which was probably a mistake.) When we got married, I thought we could handle her eating (or non-eating) problems together, but it has proven to be too much for me. If you have any words of wisdom, I am open to them.

Michael L.
Westchester, Calif.

P.S. One of my wife's problems is that she has told me on numerous occasions that she is actually jealous of my body.

Dear Michael:

Dan and I can certainly understand what you have been through. You both are obviously high achievers and probably quite competitive when it boils right down to it. My own bizarre eating rituals, deception, physical problems and the accompanying tension took a tremendous toll in our lives over a period of time. Without the intervention of a skilled psychotherapist, I am not at all certain our marriage would have worked out. But the bottom line is that we are still together due largely to the kind of expertise provided by a first-rate doctor. I'm sure you would agree that no athlete can attain world class status without a good coach. You could say the same thing about your marriage at this point. While it seems like an impossible challenge, the right type of "coaching" could produce a workable (even rewarding) relationship. Obviously, it requires unyielding commitment, perseverance and, at times, pain to take on the challenge of winning that first place medal. A far greater challenge is taking life's most important relationship and winning a "trophy" which is immeasurably greater in human terms. Don't let go too soon! Find a qualified therapist or counselor who can help you to help one another toward health and happiness. Take it from me—it can be done. What Shirley needs now, more than ever, is support, acceptance and love.

Cherry Boone O'Neill

ꭗꭗ

Dear Cherry Boone:

I feel like I am at the end of my rope and I have no one to turn to but you because I know you have recovered from your illness. Your book truly inspired me. It made me want to seek help for my anorexia and bulimia. After more than two years of therapy I feel that I can honestly say I am no longer an anorexic person. But I am having problems with bingeing and purging. I don't take laxatives very much at all any more and I finally gave up my crazy exercising schedule but I can't stop vomiting. I know it's bad for me and can damage my health. I am only nineteen years old and already I have had thousands of dollars worth of dental bills because my teeth have been affected. I feel like I am addicted to vomiting and that I cannot give up bulimia. I have tried everything but each day I face the same awful temptations. If you write to people, please give me some ideas about how you stopped bingeing and purging.

Sonia C.
Buffalo, N. Y.

Dear Sonia:

I also found bulimic behavior one of the hardest things to control in my recovery process. I seemed to be caught in a cycle of recovery and relapse but I stumbled on to something that you may find helpful. I have attempted to find something helpful to do for others each day, or at least several times a week—it helps me focus my attention outward and enables me to put my own problems in the proper perspective. At the same time, I have replaced bingeing with a daily treat or reward for myself. It is good to look forward to something every day and I look forward to spending one hour a day swimming on weekdays. Also, sometimes I will pick out a movie that I really want to see or something special to purchase. This provides me with an opportunity to give myself a loving and appropriate reward. Bingeing and purging had become an inappropriate attempt to gratify appetites which were inflated and habitually unsatisfied. Sometimes recovery involves replacing an inappropriate behavior with a more appropriate one. Healing is a gradual transition which takes time but can be accomplished. You may also want to ask your therapist about some of the latest medication which is being used to treat bulimia. Of course I don't have to tell you the dangers of continued bulimic activity—you already know them. I know you can recover and that is my hope for you.

Cherry Boone O'Neill

✄✄

Dear Cherry:

What I am about to write to you I have never told anyone except my very best friend. She is the one who said I should write to you. I am fourteen years old and I have lost a lot of weight. Almost fourteen pounds. I now weigh 91. I think I am experiencing the same thing you did. Also, last year my uncle asked me to have sex with him which I didn't but some other things did happen. I was afraid of him and afraid to tell anyone. I think I am pretty mixed up right now. How can so many things be going wrong in my life?

Tina G.
Silver Springs, Md.

Dear Tina:

It is very possible that your two problems may be related. You may be avoiding contact with your uncle by making yourself unattractive or sick. It is extremely important that you share with a school counselor or your parents about the experience you had with your uncle. Sexual abuse is an extremely serious matter. You have nothing to be ashamed of and you should not feel guilty. Your anorexia, very possibly a defense measure, may take care of itself in time. But I would strongly urge you to see a doctor before matters get worse. Thank you for sharing your story with me—that's a good first step in the right direction!

Cherry Boone O'Neill

✕✕

Dear Cherry:

I feel like I know you personally because I have read your book three times all the way through. I hope you don't mind me writing to you about my own problem. About four years ago I began losing weight by dieting. The first few pounds came off so easily that I wanted to lose more and felt very positive about myself for the first time in years. Somehow I just lost control. I am now down to 89 pounds and I finally went to see our family doctor for the first time (I refused to go earlier). Dr. D. says I am probably afraid of sex and that I fear pregnancy. This shocked me because I have always want to be married and to have a family. Could I have these fears and not know it? Dr. D.'s diagnosis makes me want to forget about my next appointment because I don't think he knows much about what I am facing. I am afraid to tell him because he has been our family doctor since I was five years old. I am now twenty.

M. McMillan
Salem, Oreg.

Dear M.:

Your family physician may not be aware of advancements made in the treatment of anorexia and other eating disorders which has evolved over the past several years. It was commonly thought, in past years, that anorexics were attempting to avoid sex, pregnancy or both. Sometimes this can be true, I have no doubt. But it can be an oversimplified explanation and many times is simply not the case. Speak with your parents about the fact that you feel you need more expert counsel in this area. You could show them this letter if you want to because I stand behind you in your doubts about your family doctor's ability to effectively treat your condition, although he may be a wonderful general practitioner. This eating disorder is too serious to guess at—you need competent medical attention, the sooner the better.

Cherry

❧❧

Dear Cherry:

As you can see by the return address on this envelope, I am writing to you from Kenya. My parents are missionaries and I have lived here for three years. Before that, we lived in Thailand. My dad is a doctor. I am seventeen years old and have already attended more schools than I can count. I have only lived in the United States a few years and most of that time was with my grandparents. I have no really good friends. A lot of the M.K.s (missionary kids) are involved in drugs and drinking and I'm not into that. I have already been hospitalized once because I was under the weight limit set by my dad, which is 100 pounds. I'm afraid it's going to happen again soon. My cousin sent me a magazine article that you wrote telling your story. I guess I would like you to share any helpful ideas you might have.

Wynn B.
Nairobi, Kenya

Dear Wynn:

I would say that you are a "good girl" who wants to have some control over her life. You probably don't want to rebel through behavior which is unacceptable to you so you are taking control of what you do have—your body. I went through much the same thing. You might feel helpless because you must move from country to country with your parents. You may also be seeking to say something to your parents which expresses itself through your eating disorder. It could be a cry for attention—perhaps you feel your parents are reaching out to help a needy world but somehow they are overlooking you. These are the kind of questions that you must explore with a qualified counselor. I don't know what conditions are like in Nairobi, Kenya, but I would suspect that there may not be many experts in the area of eating

117

disorders. This means your family will be faced with some tough choices regarding your health. Some kind of family therapy sessions would be particularly helpful in your situation, but if your parents can't commit to staying in the U.S. for an extended period of time, perhaps you could stay with your grandparents to begin treatment and have them join you when it is possible. If your father is a medical doctor he will understand the importance of dealing with your illness. I hope some of these thoughts have been helpful and have provided some hope that there are answers to be found for your problem, especially in light of all the research that is now taking place on the subject. My thoughts and prayers are with you, Wynn.

Cherry O'Neill

✕℃✕℃

Dear Cherry Boone O'Neill:

I am a thirty-seven-year-old mother of four children and a recently recovered bulimic. I have gone back to school in hopes of obtaining a degree in psychology or some other area which would help me touch people's lives in a positive way. Because you were a great inspiration to me in my recovery period, and because I know you must have done research in the area of eating disorders, I would be most interested in your views regarding American culture and eating disorders of the kind you and I experienced. What about other countries? I have been led to understand that in Eastern and European countries there are very few cases of anorexia nervosa and bulimia.

Mrs. T. C. Bowman
Mission Viejo, Calif.

Dear T.:

On the surface it would seem as though the severe eating disorders are mostly found in the West, particularly in the U.S. Indeed, anorexia and bulimia probably have a higher incidence in developed nations such as ours, however, I believe that a closer look will reveal there are the same underlying emotional needs that, if unfulfilled, can lead to problems in all human beings no matter where they are. Though I have not done extensive research, medical opinions which are informal in their evaluation seem to indicate that different cultures have their own eating disorders. For example, in certain parts of the Pacific, islanders who have eaten certain culturally accepted diets frequently become extremely obese. In Africa, there are many customs which are different than our own which impact the physiology because of certain nutritional standards. Some may be healthy but some may be extremely unhealthy. One thing is certain, more research is being done all the time in these areas—perhaps you will make a contribution! I am glad to hear of your recovery and your determination to educate yourself in preparation for work in the area of human service. Good luck!

Cherry

❧❧❧

Dear Cherry:

My husband is the pastor of a large, nondenominational charismatic church in our city. We thank God for the great success we have, including a local radio program which you may have heard about which is taped every Sunday morning in our church service. Nearly nineteen hundred people attend and we have sent out fifteen missionaries to different parts of Asia and Africa. Our only real family problem is our oldest daughter, Karen, who refuses to eat, exercises several hours a day, vomits if she has eaten too much and refuses any help. Karen and I both read your book last winter and we were wondering if you could explain a bit further what you meant by the fact that you felt like an entertainer's daughter and a preacher's daughter all at the same time. Could we be contributing to Karen's problems? We don't want our family to be a poor witness so we want to get this problem dealt with as soon as possible and, of course, we want Karen to succeed in life and be healthy.

Mrs. T. D. Kay
Oklahoma City, Okla.

Dear Mrs. Kay:

I can see that success is important to your family and your church figures strongly into the picture. I think it is important that you consider Karen's needs for who she is rather than for the image she projects in terms of a "witness." She may be crying out for attention in the midst of a family which is extremely busy helping others through Christian work. She wants to know that she counts too. I felt like a preacher's daughter because there were such high expectations on my life to be a "good girl." I was the older sister, the example, a good Christian, the picture of wholesome American life. I knew I could not measure up to these high expectations, much of which were self-imposed. Remember, Karen and your other children are always in view of the church congregation and are, essentially, on trial all the time. She might feel she's wearing an invisible straightjacket and this kind of constant pressure often brings about some type of behavioral reaction—to escape or call out for help. I hope you don't think that I am being disrespectful of your mission in the

120

church, but I think your first order of business must be your family life, which includes Karen's health. Please seek professional medical help from one who is qualified in the area of eating disorders, and be prepared to participate in some family sessions with her. This is extremely important. God bless you.

Cherry O'Neill

XCXC

Dear Cherry:

I am a member of a large church in Van Nuys, California where you and your family came to sing and speak on a Sunday evening some years ago. Of course, I have followed the Boone family and, in particular, your own story over these past years. Your book was extremely inspirational to me. A rumor has been circulating in our church and among some of my friends that you have suffered a relapse and are anorexic or bulimic once again. Someone told me that you were once again going back to your doctor for treatment. Can this be true? I didn't want to continue the rumor without checking with you. Can you tell us something about your condition? We are praying for you.

Mrs. T. B. Blakely
Sherman Oaks, Calif.

Dear Mrs. Blakely:

I'm happy to inform you that the rumor you heard is just that—a rumor. It has also come to my attention that some people believe I have had a relapse which is not true. I have indeed faced some tremendous challenges which have taken a considerable emotional toll—a hectic schedule, speaking engagements, media interviews and caring for two very active, bright children. Because my anorexia and bulimia had some relationship to a genetically transmitted mood disorder, it is important that I remain in touch with my doctor occasionally, which I have done, especially in times of extreme stress. Also, I experienced some postpartum depression after the premature birth of my son, Brendan. I'm happy to report, mother and children are doing just fine! Thank you for coming directly to me with the question. Your prayers are appreciated.

Cherry Boone O'Neill

⚬⚬⚬

Dear Mrs. O'Neill:

I am eleven years old. This is my first year in middle school. My science report is on anorexia nervosa. Would you help me by sending answers to these questions?

1. Do you feel that your parents' expectations were too high?
2. Were you ever afraid of dying?
3. What would you do if Brittany grew up and got anorexia?
4. Why couldn't you quit dieting sooner?
5. Is there a medication for anorexia nervosa?
6. Do you still diet now?
7. Did you think you were fat when you weighed 80 pounds?
8. How can people avoid anorexia?
9. Which age groups are most likely to get anorexia?

Thanks a million.

Miriam H.
Tampa, Fla.

P.S. My dad loves your dad's singing.

Dear Miriam:

That's quite a list of questions! I'll try to answer them. It's good that this subject is being dealt with by both teachers and students in schools across the nation.

1. My parents' expectations may have been high, but mine were higher, and that was a major problem.

2. There were times when my weight was down so low that I feared death, but my thinking was distorted and I was unable to think rationally of the consequences of my disorder.

3. Of course, as any parent, I would feel anxiety and concern if my daughter experienced anorexia nervosa. I believe, however, that my own experience has prepared me to take preventative measures, which are the most important. We have worked to instill a good self-image in Brittany and a freedom to accomplish things and take on responsibilities at her own speed, as we assist her in developing her own realistic expectations. We want her to love herself as we love her—unconditionally.

4. I couldn't quit dieting sooner than I did because I could no longer see myself objectively. I'd lost touch with reality. The seriousness of this eating disorder requires long-term treatment to change deeply ingrained behaviors. Healing is a *process* and must be given time to develop.

5. There are medications available which can help deal with certain causes and effects of anorexia and bulimia, but they are very different for different people and must be carefully handled under the supervision of a doctor. Increasing research is being done into the area of drug therapy. At this time, however, there is no proven pharmaceutical "cure all" for eating disorders. I, personally, doubt that there ever will be.

6. Though I am still conscious of what I eat, and will change my intake from time to time for nutritional reasons,

I do not design programs to lose weight. I am not tempted to diet or to binge, but rather I have found a good weight for my body and I seem to maintain this weight with little effort.

7. I actually had two major bouts with anorexia during my ten-year battle with eating disorders. The first time I got down to 92 pounds through strict dieting and rigorous exercise. Although now I can see that I was skeletal at that weight, then I was proud of my lean, well-toned reflection in the mirror. The second time, however, when I plunged to 80 pounds as a result of laxative abuse and vomiting, I knew I looked awful, but the fear of getting fat was more powerful than my desire to look better. I know it all sounds incredible but one's body image as well as realistic perception of values and fears become radically and increasingly distorted if this affliction goes untreated.

8. People can avoid anorexia nervosa by developing identities which do not depend on other people's expectations. It is important that we develop a certain independence from society's demands on our body images and the expectation of others that we fit certain stereotypes. On the other hand, there are some people who will inevitably fall victim to these kinds of disorders because of environmental and genetic predispositions.

9. It would seem as though most cases of anorexia nervosa are concentrated in the teenage years although now there is evidence that it is spreading to younger groups and to those much older.

Good luck on your report!

Cherry Boone O'Neill

✕

Dear Cherry:

I am a twenty-one-year-old college student and have been fighting to overcome anorexia and bulimia over the past four years. I recently saw you on a TV news program and I read your book so I have some idea of what you have been through. It is encouraging to know that others have gone before me and have recovered. My problem is, I have spent literally tens of thousands of dollars (I should say my family has) on treatment. I'm feeling guilty and I know that funds are running low. I guess the real reason I am writing is to ask you if you've heard of a new drug treatment which is a kind of "miracle cure" for anorexia and bulimia. I believe this treatment involves brain biochemistry and I have heard the results are remarkable and fast. Do you know anything about this? It sounds almost too good to be true.

Patricia J.
Orlando, Fla.

Dear Patricia:

If something sounds too good to be true, it probably is. I, too, have heard that there are certain "quick fix" claims being made and I would urge great caution in falling victim to an overly simplistic answer to an extremely complex problem. I personally feel that it is essential that a comprehensive and integrated program of psychotherapy, nutrition and medication (if needed) be followed under the close supervision of qualified experts if recovery is to be complete and permanent. I have said many times that, just as it takes months or years to develop eating disorders, it can take months or years to emerge from them. Instant cures almost invariably lead to disappointment.

Cherry O'Neill

P.S. How timely! I just received "The Hopeline Newsletter"

from Kim Lampson (volume 4, number 3 September 30, 1984). She covers the subject of quick cures—good luck!*

The following are letters from recovered anorexics and bulimics. I hope this provides further hope to those who are still finding their way.

Cherry

Dear Cherry:

I can't believe you actually answered my letter! Thank you so much. I took your advice and began seeing a doctor who specializes in eating disorders and I know that I can get well. At long last there is light at the end of the tunnel. Thanks for the inspiration and the words of wisdom.

Ruthel A.
Anchorage, Alaska

Dear Cherry:

Reading your book, *Starving for Attention,* was awful for me because I saw myself on every page. In some ways, it was almost as if someone were writing my own story, even down to certain details. I couldn't believe you would actually make

* See Bibliography for addresses of newsletters.

yourself vulnerable and tell everything about your illness. I read your book twice, then, for the first time in my life, I gained the courage to actually tell someone about my problem. Within a few days I was seeing a doctor and I am now on the road to recovery. I have never felt better about myself. Thank you for sharing your story. I know it must have been difficult.

Victoria C.
Vancouver, B.C.

Dear Mrs. O'Neill:

I can't tell you how much your story has meant to me personally. Just to know there was someone else in the world going through what I was going through became an immeasurable source of comfort to me. I wasn't such a freak after all! Your book not only helped me to come out in the open with my problem, but helped two of my girlfriends at school to get into counseling for their own eating problems. We saw you on a television program talking about your book. They showed before and after pictures, which were hard to believe, but which were the proof I needed to face recovery. I can't tell you how difficult it has been but I know now that I can overcome my problems.

Estelle P.
San Bernardino, Calif.

Dear Cherry:

It has been more than a year since I received your letter. If you will remember, I had stopped seeing my doctor because I didn't feel he was really helping me. Now I know that I just didn't want to be helped. I didn't want anybody intruding into my own world of power and control. Your note really gave me food for thought. I didn't know how really serious bulimia could be and it really made me think about what I was doing. When I finally decided to get well, I went back to my doctor, as you recommended. It was harder to overcome than I ever thought it could be, but I have managed to gain fifteen pounds and to feel much better about myself. I appreciate your concern.

Sue Ellen S.
Atlanta, Ga.

Dear Cherry:

You may not remember, but my mother, Betty M., wrote you a letter last year when I was in the hospital. She asked you to call and, thank God, you did. You didn't even know me and you certainly didn't have to make a long distance phone call. I could barely talk and there is a lot I don't remember about the call but I do know that it saved my life. I couldn't believe you would care for a stranger. My weight was down to 64 pounds and I had been hospitalized for more than a month. I could have died but you gave me hope. I now weigh 100 pounds and even though I sometimes have a minor relapse, I am much better. How can I ever find the words to thank you? Thank you for caring!

Sylvia M.
Pittsburgh, Pa.

Dear Cherry:

Last spring President Reagan called me on the telephone. I had written him a letter about my anorexia. I was really down and everything seemed so hopeless. I couldn't believe it when the White House called with words of encouragement. I guess he does that sometimes. Well, as you know, a White House staff person contacted your husband to put you in touch with me and that's when you called. I just wanted to keep you posted on my progress. I believe I have fully recovered. I have put on twelve pounds and I am back in school working toward my degree in psychology. You were quite an inspiration to me and I am very thankful that you took the time to contact me, even though we had never met. Like you, I am now reaching out to others with the message that eating disorders can be overcome with the right help. I hope we can stay in touch in the future.

Margaret K.
Miami, Fla.

Dear Cherry:

I am just writing to let you know that, like you, I am a recovered bulimic. I want to support what I heard you say recently in a radio program which had to do with eating disorders. You mentioned depression and related mood disorders as possibilities in this illness. As it turned out, that's exactly what happened to me. I am now on medication which helps me with depression. I have had very few occurrences of bulimic behavior since discovering this problem. It's like a new life for me! Thank you for sharing this information. I'm sure that many people will probably be helped.

Mrs. D. V.
Seattle, Wash.

Dear Cherry Boone O'Neill:

I am a recovering anorexic. I have never gone through anything like this in my life and for the longest time I had no hope that I would get better. I guess the most important thing you said in your letter was that recovering from this kind of disorder takes a long time. You called it a process. Without that reassurance I could not have carried on. It seemed like there was no end to it at all. I even thought about suicide. But now I feel much better. There are times when I fall back into old patterns or when I experience fear as weight goes on, but at least now I know that over a period of time I have truly gotten better and that some day I will be completely well. Thank you for the encouragement and continue to let others know that we can win this battle.

Rebecca Q.
Phoenix, Ariz.

Bibliography

Books on Anorexia Nervosa and Bulimia

Boskind-White, Marlene, and William C. White, Jr. *Bulimarexia: The Binge/Purge Cycle*. Norton, 1983.

Brunch, Hilde. *Eating Disorders: Obesity, Anorexia Nervosa, and the Person Within*. Basic Books, 1973.

———. *The Golden Cage: The Enigma of Anorexia Nervosa*. Harvard University Press, 1978.

Cauwels, Janice M. *Bulimia: The Binge Purge Compulsion*. Doubleday, 1983.

Chernin, Kim. *The Obsession: Reflections on the Tyranny of Slenderness*. Harper and Row, 1981.

Crisp, Arthur H. *Anorexia Nervosa: Let Me Be*. Academic Press, Grune and Stratton, 1980.

Dally, Peter, and Joan Gomez. *Obesity and Anorexia Nervosa: A Question of Shape*. Faber & Faber, 1980.

Garfinkel, Paul E., and David M. Garner. *Anorexia Nervosa: A Multidimensional Perspective*. Brunner/Mazel, 1982.

Gross, Meier, ed. *Anorexia Nervosa*. D. C. Heath, Collamore Press, 1982.

Havekamp, Katharina. *The Empty Face*. Richard Marek Publisher, 1978.

Heater, Sandra H. *Am I Still Visible?* Betterway, 1983.

Hudlow, Emily Ellison. *Alabaster Chambers*. St. Martin's Press, 1980.

Josephs, Rebecca, *Early Disorder*. Farrar, Straus & Giroux, 1979.

Landau, Elaine. *Why Are They Starving Themselves?* Messner, 1983.

Latimer, Jane Evans. *Reflections on Recovery: Freedom from Bulimia and Compulsive Overeating*. Mesa Productions, 1983.

Levenkron, Steven. *The Best Little Girl in the World*. Contemporary Books, 1978.

———. *Treating and Overcoming Anorexia Nervosa*. Scribner, 1982; Warner, 1983.

Liu, Aimee. *Solitaire*. Harper and Row, 1979.

MacLeod, Sheila. *The Art of Starvation: A Story of Anorexia and Survival*. Schocken Books, 1982.

Minuchin, Salvador, Bernice L. Rosman, and Lester Baker. *Psychosomatic Families: Anorexia Nervosa in Context*. Harvard University Press, 1978.

Neuman, Patricia A., and Patricia A. Halvorson. *Anorexia Nervosa and Bulimia: A Handbook for Counselors and Therapists*. Van Nostrand Rheinhold, 1983.

O'Neill, Cherry Boone. *Starving for Attention*. Continuum, 1982.

Palazzoli, Mara Selvini. *Self-Starvation: From Individual to Family Therapy in the Treatment of Anorexia Nervosa*. Jason Aronson, 1978; Human Context Books, Caucer, 1974.

Palmer, R. E. *Anorexia Nervosa*. Penguin, 1980.

Pope, Harrison G., and James I. Hudson. *New Hope for Binge Eaters*. Harper and Row, 1984.

Roth, Geneen. *Feeding the Hungry Heart: The Experience of Compulsive Eating*. Bobbs-Merrill, 1982.

Rumny, Auis. *Dying to Please: Anorexia Nervosa and Its Cure*. McFarland, 1983.

Sours, John A. *Starving to Death in a Sea of Objects: The Anorexia Nervosa Syndrome*. Jason Aronson, 1980.

Sperling, Melitta. *Psychosomatic Disorders in Childhood*. Jason Aronson, 1978.

Squire, Susan. *The Slender Balance*. Putnam, 1983.

Thoma, Helmut. *Anorexia Nervosa*. International Universities Press, 1967.

Vigersky, Robert. *Anorexia Nervosa*. Raven Press, 1977.

Vincent, L. M. *Competing with the Sylph: The Pursuit of the Ideal Body Form*. Berkeley Books, 1979, paperback.

Wilson, Charles Philip, Charles C. Hogan, and Ira L. Mintz. *The Fear of Being Fat: The Treatment of Anorexia and Bulimia*. Jason Aronson, 1983.

Books on Related Subjects

Bennett, William G., and Joel Gurin. *Dieter's Dilemma: Eating Less and Weighing More*. Basic Books, 1982.

Burns, David D. *Feeling Good*. New American Library, 1981.

Bloom, Lynn, et al. *The New Assertive Woman*. Dell paperback, 1975.

Briggs, Dorothy Corkille. *Celebrate Yourself: Making Life Work for You*. Doubleday, 1977.

———. *Your Child's Self-Esteem*. Doubleday, 1970.

Kuntzleman, Charles. *Diet Free: The No-Diet Way to a Beautiful Body.* Rodale Press, 1981.

Millman, Marcia. *Such a Pretty Face: Being Fat in America.* Norton, 1980.

Napier, Augustus, and Carl Whitaker. *The Family Crucible.* Bantam paperback, 1978.

Orbach, Suzie. *Fat Is a Feminist Issue.* Paddington Press, Medallion Books, 1978.

Powell, Pauline S. *Obesity: The Regulation of Weight.* Williams and Wilkins, 1980.

Satir, Virginia. *Conjoint Family Therapy.* Science and Behavior Books, 1967.

Vath, Raymond E., and Daniel W. O'Neill. *Marrying for Life.* Winston Press, 1982.

Zales, Michael R., ed. *Eating, Sleeping and Sexuality.* Brunner/Mazel, 1982.

Articles

Bassoe, H., and I. Eskeland. "A Prospective Study of 133 Patients with Anorexia Nervosa Treatment and Outcome." *Acta Psychiatrica Scandinavica,* February 1982, vol. 65, no. 2, pp. 127–33.

Boskind-Lodahl, Marlene. "Cinderella's Stepsisters: A Feminist Perspective on Anorexia Nervosa and Bulimia." *Psychology of Women Selected Readings,* pp. 436–48. W. W. Norton and Co., 1979.

Boskind-Lodahl, Marlene, and William C. White, Jr. "The Definition and Treatment of Bulimarexia in College Women—A Pilot Study." *Journal of American College Health Association,* October 1978, vol. 27, no. 2.

———. "Group Therapy with Bulimarexic Women," National Conference on Eating Disorders, University of Maine, 1980.

Bourget, B., and D. R. White. "Performance of Overweight and Normal-Weight Girls on Delay of Gratification Tasks," *International Journal of Eating Disorders,* Spring 1984, vol. 3, no. 3.

Brotman, A. W., D. B. Herzog, and S. W. Woods. "Antidepressant Treatment of Bulimia: The Relationship Between Bingeing and Depressive Symptomatology," *The Journal of Clinical Psychiatry,* January 1984, vol. 45, no. 1, pp. 7–9.

Bruch, Hilde. "Anorexia Nervosa," *Nutrition Today,* September–October 1978.

———. "Anorexia Nervosa: A Review," *Ross Timesaver, Dietetic Currents,* March–April 1977, vol. 4, no. 2.

133

———. "The Enigma of Anorexia Nervosa," *Medical Times,* May 1976, vol. 104, No. 5.

———. "Perils of Behavior Modification in Treatment of Anorexia Nervosa," *Journal of the American Medical Association,* 9 December 1974, vol. 230, no. 10.

———. "Treatment in Anorexia Nervosa," *International Journal of Psychoanalytic Psychotherapy,* vol. 9, pp. 303–12.

Cantwell, Dennis, Susan Sturzenberger, Jane Burroughs, Barbara Salkin, and Jacquelyn K. Breen. "Anorexia Nervosa: An Affective Disorder," *Archives of General Psychiatry,* September 1977, vol. 34.

Casper, Regina, and John M. Davis. "On the Course of Anorexia Nervosa," *American Journal of Psychiatry,* September 1977.

deRosa, G., et al. "Endocrine Study of Anorexia Nervosa," *Exp. Clin. Endocrinology,* August 1983, vol. 82, no. 2, pp. 160–72.

———. "Thyroid Function in Altered Nutritional State," *Exp. Clin. Endocrinology,* August 1983, vol. 82, no. 2, pp. 173–77.

Dixon, Katharine, and James Falko. "Benign Parotid Enlargement in Bulimia," *Annals of Internal Medicine,* December 1980.

Epling, W. F., W. D. Pierce, and L. Stefan. "A Theory of Activity-Based Anorexia," *The International Journal of Eating Disorders,* Autumn 1983, vol. 3, no. 1.

Fairburn, C., and P. J. Cooper. "The Clinical Features of Bulimia Nervosa," *British Journal of Psychology,* March 1984, vol. 144, pp. 238–46.

Frankenberg, F. R. Hoarding. "Anorexia Nervosa," *British Journal of Medical Psychology,* March 1984, vol. 57, no. 1, pp. 57–60.

Gandour, M. J. "Bulimia: Clinical Description, Assessment, Etiology and Treatment," *International Journal of Eating Disorders,* Spring 1984, vol. 3, no.3.

Garner, David, et al. "A Multidimensional Psychotherapy for Anorexia Nervosa," *International Journal of Eating Disorders,* Winter 1982, vol. 1, no. 2.

Gwirtsaman, H. E., et al. "Bulimia in Men: A Report of Three Cases," *Journal of Clinical Psychiatry,* February 1984, vol. 45, no. 2, pp. 78–81.

Hogan, William M., Enrique Huerta, and Alexander Lucas. "Diagnosing Anorexia Nervosa in Males," *Psychosomatics,* vol. 15.

Kagan, D. M., and R. L. Squires. "Dieting, Compulsive Eating and Feelings of Failure among Adolescents," *The International Journal of Eating Disorders,* Autumn 1983, vol. 3, no. 1.

Katz, M. A., et al. "The Prevalence of Frequent Binge Eating and Bulimia in a Non-clinical College Example," *International Journal of Eating Disorders,* Spring 1984, vol. 3, no. 3.

Kaufer, J. F., and J. L. Katz. "Rorschach Responses in Anorectic and Nonanorectic Women," *The International Journal of Eating Disorders,* Autumn 1983, vol. 3, no. 1.

Larocca, F. E. F. "Gilles-de-la-Tourettes (The Movement Disorder): The Association with a Case of Anorexia Nervosa in a Boy," *International Journal of Eating Disorders,* Spring 1984, vol. 3, no. 3

Lerner, H. D. "Contemporary Psychoanalytic Perspectives on Gorge-Vomiting: A Case Illustration," *International Journal of Eating Disorders,* Autumn 1983, vol. 3, no. 1.

Loeb, Margaret. "How to Stop the New Splurge/Purge Diet Problems," *US,* 30 October 1979.

Lucas, Alexander. "Anorexia Nervosa," *Contemporary Nutrition,* August 1978, vol. 3, no. 8, General Mills Nutrition Department.

————. "Bulimia and Vomiting Syndrome," *Contemporary Nutrition,* April 1981, vol. 6, no. 4.

Maloney, Michael J., and Michael K. Farrell. "Treatment of Severe Weight Loss in Anorexia Nervosa with Hyperalimentation and Psychotherapy," *American Journal of Psychiatry,* March 1980, vol. 137, no. 3.

McNab, W. L. "Anorexia and the Adolescent," *J. School Health,* September 1983, vol. 53, no. 7, pp. 427–30.

Minuchin, Salvador. "A Conceptual Model of Psychosomatic Illness in Children," *Archives of General Psychiatry,* August 1975, vo. 32.

Mitchell, James, and Richard Pyle. "The Bulimic Syndrome in Normal Weight Individuals: A Review," *International Journal of Eating Disorders,* Winter 1982, vol. 1, no. 2.

Morgan, H. G., and J. Welbourne Purgold. "Management and Outcome in Anorexia Nervosa: A Standardized Prognostic Study," *British Journal of Psychiatry,* September 1983, vol. 143, pp. 282–87.

Mushatt, Cecil. "Anorexia Nervosa: A Psychoanalytic Commentary," *International Journal of Psychoanalytic Psychotherapy,* vol. 9.

Ong, Y. L., S. A. Checkley, and G. F. Russell. "Suppression of Bulimic Symptoms with Methyl Amphetamine," *British Journal of Psychiatry,* September 1983, vol. 143, pp. 288–93.

Pope, H. G., and J. I. Hudson. "Anorexia and Bulimia among 300 Suburban Women Shoppers," *American Journal of Psychiatry,* February 1984, vol. 141, no. 2, pp. 292–94.

Pope, H. G., J. I. Hudson, and J. M. Jonas. "Anti-Depressant Treatment of Bulimia: Preliminary Experience and Practical Recommendations," *J. Clin Psychopharm.,* October 1983, vol. 3, no. 5, pp. 274–81.

Pope, H. G., and J. I. Hudson, et al. "Prevalence of Anorexia Nervosa and Bulimia in Three Student Populations," *International Journal of Eating Disorders,* Spring 1984, vol. 3, no. 3.

Price, William A., and Jame Giannini, "Binge Eating During Menstruation," "Letter to the Editor," *The Journal of Clinical Psychiatry*, November 1983, vol. 4, no. 11, p. 431.

Pumariega, A. J., P. Edward, and C. B. Mitchell. "Anorexia Nervosa in Black Adolescents," *Journal of American Academy of Child Psychiatry*, 1984, vol. 23, no. 1, pp. 111–14.

Rockwell, W., E. H. Ellinwood, Jr., and D. W. Trader. "Psychotropic Drugs Promoting Weight Gain: Health Risks and Treatment Implications," Review Article, *Southern Medical Journal*, November 1983, vol. 78, no. 11, pp. 1407–12.

Schwabe, Arthur, et al. "Anorexia Nervosa," *Annals of Internal Medicine*, vol. 94, pp. 371–81.

———. "Anorexia Nervosa and Bulimia: The Sociocultural Context," *International Journal of Eating Disorders*, Spring 1982, vol. 1. no. 3.

Silverman, J. A., and Richard Morton. "Limner of Anorexia Nervosa: His Life and Times," *Journal of the American Medical Association*, 25 November 1983, vol. 250, no. 20, pp. 2830–32.

Silverman, J. A. "The Cambridge Diet: More Mayhem?" *Journal of the American Medical Association*, 25 November 1983, vol. 250, no. 20, pp. 2833–34.

Sitnick, T., and J. L. Katz. "Sex Role Identity and Anorexia Nervosa," *International Journal of Eating Disorders*, Spring 1984, vol. 3, no. 3.

Smali, A., J. Madero, et al. "Intellect, Perceptual Characteristics, and Weight Gain in Anorexia Nervosa," *J. Clin. Psychology*, September 1983, vol. 39, no. 5, pp. 780–82.

Solvom, L., R. Freeman, et al. "The Comparative Psychopathology of Anorexia Nervosa: Obsessive-Compulsive Disorder or Phobia?" *International Journal of Eating Disorders*, Autumn 1983, vol. 3, no. 1.

Srikameswaran, S., et al. "Sex Role Ideology among Women with Anorexia Nervosa and Bulimia," *International Journal of Eating Disorders*, Spring 1984, vol. 3, no. 3.

Stern, Steven, et al. "Anorexia Nervosa: The Hospital's Role in Family Treatment," *Family Process*, December 1981, vol. 20, no. 4.

Story, Ian. "Anorexia Nervosa and the Psychotherapeutic Hospital," *International Journal of Psychoanalytic Psychotherapy*, vol. 9.

Swartz, J. "Bulimia: The Obsession to Be Thin," *Canadian Medical Association Journal*, 1 April 1984, vol. 130, no. 7, pp. 923–24.

Swift, W. J., et al. "Ego Development in Anorexia Inpatients," *International Journal of Eating Disorders*, Spring 1984, vol. 3. no. 3.

Touyz, S. W., and P. J. Beaumont, et al., "Body Shape Perception and Its Disturbance in Anorexia Nervosa," *British Journal of Psychiatry*, February 1984, vol. 144, pp. 166–71.

Vandereycken, W. "Neuroleptics in the Short-Term Treatment of Anorexia Nervosa. A Double-Blind Placebo-Control Study with Sulpiride," *British Journal of Psychiatry,* March 1984, vol. 144, pp. 288–92.

Walsh, Timothy. "The Endocrinology of Anorexia Nervosa," *Psychiatric Clinics of North America,* August 1980, vol. 3, no. 2.

Warren, Michelle, and Raymond Vande Wiele. "Clinical and Metabolic Features of Anorexia Nervosa," *American Journal of Obstetrics and Gynecology,* 1 October 1973.

White, M. "Anorexia Nervosa: A Transgenerational System Perspective," *Family Process,* September 1983, vol. 22, no. 3, pp. 255–73.

Wilson, Philip, "The Fear of Being Fat and Anorexia Nervosa," *International Journal of Psychoanalytic Psychotherapy,* vol. 9.

Wooley, Wayne, and Susan Wooley. "Editorial: The Beverly Hills Eating Disorder: The Mass Marketing of Anorexia Nervosa." *International Journal of Eating Disorders,* Spring 1982, vol. 1, no.3.

Newsletters

American Anorexia Nervosa Association, Inc.
133 Cedar Lane
Teaneck, NJ 07666
(201) 836-1800

ANRED ALERT: Anorexia Nervosa
and Related Eating Disorders, Inc.
P. O. Box 5102
Eugene, OR 97405
(503) 344-1144

B.A.S.H., Inc.: Bulimia Anorexia Self-Help
621 S. New Ballas Road
St. Louis, MO 63141
(314) 567-4080

The Hopeline
550 16th Avenue
Suite 301
Seattle, WA 98122

NAAS: National Anorexic Aid Society, Inc.
P. O. Box 29461
Columbus, OH 43229
(614) 895-2009